BRA

WHO DONE IT?
PUZZLES

pil

Publications International, Ltd.

Louis Weber, CEO
Publications International, Ltd.
8140 Lehigh Avenue
Morton Grove, IL 60053

ISBN: 978-1-63938-002-2

Manufactured in China.

8 7 6 5 4 3 2 1

Let's get social!

@Publications_International

@PublicationsInternational

@BrainGames.TM

www.pilbooks.com

CAN YOU FIGURE OUT WHO DID IT?

Did you want to be a detective when you were a kid? Do you read mystery novels and know the culprit before page 25? If so, this is the book for you! The mind stretchers in this book will let you pit your deductive skills against more than 150 puzzles.

You'll find a variety of puzzles here. Some will test your logical acumen, others your memory, others your observational skills. You'll have to remember what you saw in crime scene photographs, crack codes to reveal intercepted messages, solve logic puzzles to find where the thief is, and more. You'll solve some mysteries with bursts of inspiration, while others will require harder work. Themed crosswords and word searches will remind you of your favorite true crime cases and fictional dramas.

Don't worry if you find yourself getting stuck from time to time. Answers are located at the back of the book when you need a helpful boost.

So when you're ready to untangle anagrams, crack cryptograms, and track down criminals, just open the book to any page and start solving!

CRIME ABBREVIATIONS AND ACRONYMS

Answer each question below.

1. What does RICO Act stand for?

   A. Racketeer Influenced and Corrupt Organizations
   B. Racketeering Investigations and Crime Organizations
   C. Racketeering, Infiltration, and Corrupt Ownership
   D. Real Investigation of Corporate Organizations

2. What does SWAT stand for?

   A. Special Weaponry Analysis Team
   B. Special Weapons, Assaults, Tactics
   C. Special Weapons and Tactics
   D. Surge Weaponry and Targets

3. What does NCIC stand for?

   A. National Criminal Investigations Coordination
   B. National Coordination of Criminal Investigation
   C. National Crime Information Center
   D. Notorious Criminal Investigation Commission

4. What does AFIS stand for?

   A. Automated Fingerprint Identification Systems
   B. Automatic Forensics Identification Systems
   C. All-purpose Fingerprint Investigation System
   D. Automated Fingerprint Investigation Systems

Answers on page 230.

FIRST STEAL, THEN FLEE

Change just one letter on each line to go from the top word to the bottom word. Do not change the order of the letters. You must have a common English word at each step.

STEAL

steel

steep

sleep

sleet

fleet

FLEES

Answers on page 230.

FITTING WORDS

In this miniature crossword, the clues are listed randomly and are numbered for convenience only. It is up to you to figure out the placement of the 9 answers. To help you, we've inserted one letter in the grid, and this is the only occurrence of that letter in the completed puzzle.

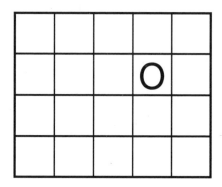

CLUES

1. Flung

2. Flung

3. Sly

4. Consumer

5. Bad lighting?

6. Was in on

7. Crime _____

8. Seal in one's bathroom

9. Solitary

Answers on page 230.

LAW AND DISORDER

While the sheriff was lost in thought about cattle rustlers and train robberies, a guy in a black hat sneaked into his office and changed a few things. Can you find all 9 changes?

Answers on page 230.

CRIME SCENE

ACROSS

1. No place for a roller skate
6. Football or badminton
11. One-named author of "A Dog of Flanders"
12. Jouster's protection
13. It's collected at a crime scene
15. Countess's counterpart
16. Ending with Vietnam or Japan
17. "But of course!"
20. "Naked Maja" painter
22. Sheriffs and marshals, e.g.
24. After-dinner treat
28. "Precious bodily fluid" that may be found at a crime scene
29. Telltale strand that may be found at a crime scene
30. Realtor sign add-on
31. Slangy physician
32. "Good gravy!"
34. It's above the horizon
35. Belonging to the Thing?
38. Metals in the raw
40. They provide a permanent record of a crime scene
45. Font feature
46. Fields of expertise
47. Jets, to Sharks
48. Garment size

DOWN

1. Fastest way to a new lawn
2. Large cask for wine
3. Org. for Saarinen
4. Concept for Colette
5. Devastated
6. "I'm sorry to say..."
7. Canada's Grand ____ National Historic Park
8. Everything: Lat.
9. Fabled giant birds
10. Sequoia or sycamore

14. Fe, to a chemist
17. Church robes
18. Metaphor for purity
19. Derelict GI
21. Between
23. Pop music's Depeche___
25. Bird of the Nile
26. Giraffe's trademark
27. Homer's besieged city
29. FBI part
31. "CSI" star Helgenberger

33. He was originally called Dippy Dawg
35. ___ dixit (unproven assertion)
36. Back in those days
37. Aching
39. "Love Song" singer Bareilles
41. Bob Cratchit's son
42. Miles ___ hour
43. Crone
44. Direction opposite NNW

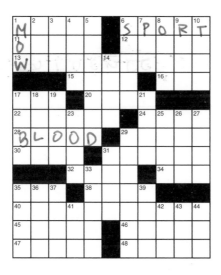

Answers on page 230.

A BLOODY DEATH

Use the clues to change just one letter on each line to go from the top word to the bottom word. Do not change the order of the letters. You must have a common English word at each step.

VEIN

VEIL   lift it to kiss the bride

VEAL   meat of calves

REAL   genuine

REAP   ...what you sow"

LEAP   a common word for bound

LEAD   ...and they will follow

DEAD

Answers on page 231.

ORDER IN THE COURT

The letters in ACQUITTAL can be found in boxes 1, 3, 4, 5, 14, 15, and 20, but not necessarily in that order. Similarly, the letters in all these words can be found in the boxes indicated. Your task is to insert all the letters of the alphabet into the boxes. If you do this correctly, the shaded cells will reveal another legal term.

Hint: Compare BAILIFF and PLAINTIFF to get the value of B, then BAILIFF to ACQUITTAL to get the value of F.

ACQUITTAL: 1, 3, 4, 5, 14, 15, 20

BAILIFF: 3, 4, 5, 17, 21
(handwritten: I, B, P)

CASE: 4, 6, 7, 20
(handwritten: A E C)

COURTROOM: 1, 2, 12, 14, 18, 20

DOCKET: 1, 7, 16, 18, 20, 26
(handwritten: K)

EXECUTION: 1, 3, 11, 17, 18, 20

GAVEL: 4, 5, 7, 22, 24
(handwritten: A)

HUNG JURY: 2, 10, 11, 13, 14, 22, 23

JUDGE: 7, 10, 14, 16, 22
(handwritten: E)

LAWYER: 2, 4, 5, 7, 13, 25
(handwritten: E)

OBJECTION: 1, 3, 7, 10, 11, 17, 18, 20
(handwritten: E)

OYEZ: 7, 8, 13, 18
(handwritten: E)

PLAINTIFF: 1, 3, 4, 5, 11, 19, 21

VERDICTS: 1, 2, 3, 6, 7, 16, 20, 24
(handwritten: is E, C)

1	2	3	4	5	6	7	8	9	10	11	12	13
		I	A			S	E	Z				Y

14	15	16	17	18	19	20	21	22	23	24	25	26
			B			C	F			V		K

Answers on page 231.

11

SPY SCRAMBLE

You're tracking down a mole, and you've found a list of
5 cities and times when the mole's flight will arrive in that
city—but the information for each meetup is scrambled
together. The letters are in order but not consecutive. Can
you decipher the cities and times?

1. BLUAESNOTSFALIIRGEHST
   Where: _____
   When: _____

2. SISNUGNARPIOSREE
   Where: _____
   When: _____

3. ELSEYVDNEENYAM
   Where: _____
   When: _____

4. MCHIIDCNAIGGHOT
   Where: _____
   When: _____

5. FIJFTOHEENAHUNNDNEREDSHBOUURRGS
   Where: _____
   When: _____

Answers on page 231.

MOTEL HIDEOUT

A thief hides out in one of the 45 motel rooms listed in the chart below. The motel's in-house detective received a sheet of four clues, signed "The Logical Thief." Using these clues, the detective found the room number within 15 minutes—but by that time, the thief had fled. Can you find the thief's motel room quicker?

1. Both digits are odd. ✓

2. The first digit is equal to or greater than the second digit.

3. The sum of the digits is 5 or less.

4. The first digit is not divisible by 3.

51	52	53	54	55	56	57	58	59
41	42	43	44	45	46	47	48	49
31	32	33	34	35	36	37	38	39
21	22	23	24	25	26	27	28	29
11	12	13	14	15	16	17	18	19

Answer on page 231.

THE SOPRANOS

Every word listed is contained within the group of letters. Words can be found in a straight line horizontally, vertically, or diagonally. They may be read either forward or backward.

ADULTERY

ANGER

ANXIETY

BOUNDARIES

CARMELA

CRIME

DEPRESSION

DRUGS

DUTIES

FOOD

LEGACY

MELFI

MONEY

NEW JERSEY

PRISON

PROTECTION

TENSION

TONY

VIOLENCE

WILLOW

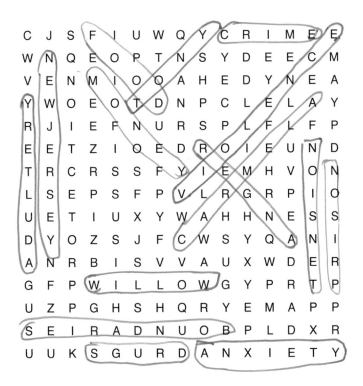

C	J	S	F	I	U	W	Q	Y	C	R	I	M	E	E
W	N	Q	E	O	P	T	N	S	Y	D	E	E	C	M
V	E	N	M	I	O	Q	A	H	E	D	Y	N	E	A
Y	W	O	E	O	T	D	N	P	C	L	E	L	A	Y
R	J	I	E	F	N	U	R	S	P	L	F	L	F	P
E	E	T	Z	I	O	E	D	R	O	I	E	U	N	D
T	R	C	R	S	S	F	Y	I	E	M	H	V	O	N
L	S	E	P	S	F	P	V	L	R	G	R	P	I	O
U	E	T	I	U	X	Y	W	A	H	H	N	E	S	S
D	Y	O	Z	S	J	F	C	W	S	Y	Q	A	N	I
A	N	R	B	I	S	V	V	A	U	X	W	D	E	R
G	F	P	W	I	L	L	O	W	G	Y	P	R	T	P
U	Z	P	G	H	S	H	Q	R	Y	E	M	A	P	P
S	E	I	R	A	D	N	U	O	B	P	L	D	X	R
U	U	K	S	G	U	R	D	A	N	X	I	E	T	Y

Answers on page 231.

TYPES OF EVIDENCE
PART I

Read the information below about forensic evidence, then turn the page.

1. **Tool marks:** If you use any sort of object to commit your crime—a pickax on a door lock, a ladder to reach a window, a knife or a rag (for any purpose)—it will be traceable. Tools used in any capacity create tiny nicks that can be detected, identified, and tracked by a crime scene investigator.

2. **Paint:** A paint chip left at a crime scene reveals volumes. If it's from the vehicle you used in committing the crime, it indicates the make and model. If paint is found on the tool you used to break into a house, it could place you at the scene. Think it's too hard to distinguish specific paint colors? There are 40,000 types of paint classified in police databases.

3. **Broken glass:** Microscopic glass fragments cling to your clothes and can't be laundered out easily. Crime labs examine tint, thickness, density, and refractive index of the fragments to determine their origins.

4. **Dust and dirt:** Even if you're a neat-and-tidy sort of criminal, dust and dirt are often missed by the most discerning eye. These particles can reveal where you live and work and if you have a pet (and what kind). If you've trudged through fields or someone's backyard, researchers can use palynology—the science that studies plant spores, insects, seeds, and other microorganisms—to track you down.

5. **Fibers:** The sources include clothing, drapes, wigs, carpets, furniture, blankets, pets, and plants. Using a compound microscope, an analyst can determine if the fibers are manufactured or natural. There are more than a thousand known fibers, as well as several thousand dyes, so if an exact match is found, you will be too.

6. **Blood:** A victim's blood tells investigators a lot, but they're also looking for different kinds of blood—including yours if you were injured at the scene—and the patterns of blood distribution. Don't bother to clean up any blood, because investigators use special lights that reveal your efforts.

7. **Bodily fluids:** Saliva, urine, vomit, and semen are a crime-scene investigator's dream, providing DNA evidence that will implicate even the most savvy criminal.

8. **Fingerprints:** One of the best ways to identify a criminal is through fingerprints left at the scene, even partial, smeared ones. Investigators enter fingerprint evidence into national databases.

9. **Shoe prints:** If you have feet (and assuming you're not a "barefoot burglar"), you left behind shoe prints. The particular treads on the soles of shoes make them easy to trace, and the bottoms of most shoes have nicks or scratches that make them easy to identify.

10. **Hair:** Humans shed a lot of hair from all parts of their bodies, so bald bandits have no advantage. Hairs as tiny as eyelashes and eyebrows have unique characteristics that reveal a lot about a person, including race, dietary habits, and overall health.

TYPES OF EVIDENCE PART II

(Do not read this until you have read the previous page!)

1. There are 40,000 types of paint classified in police databases.

    _____ True
    _____ False

2. The study of fibers is called palynology.

    _____ True
    _____ False

3. Investigators can only lift perfect fingerprints.

    _____ True
    _____ False

4. A bald criminal could still be convicted on evidence of hair.

    _____ True
    _____ False

5. Broken glass cannot easily be laundered out of clothes.

    _____ True
    _____ False

Answers on page 231.

FIND THE WITNESS

On Webster Street, there are 5 identical houses. You need to gather a witness statement from Savannah Jenkins, but you are not sure which house to approach. You know that Jenkins lives by herself but that she was out walking her dog when she saw the crime. The staff at the coffee shop around the corner give you some clues. From the information given, can you find the right house?

a. One barista says she has heard barking from houses A and C when she walks past them.

b. Another barista know the single woman who lives in house D has allergies that keep her from owning any pets.

c. The coffee shop's manager says that a retired couple lives in house C. They consider the kids who live in the house next door to them "honorary grandkids."

d. The coffee shop's manager also says that the retired couple on the other side of the family wish the kids wouldn't trek across their lawn to get to the park.

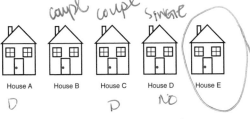

House A   House B   House C   House D   House E

Answer on page 231.

WEAPON WORDS

Add one word to each of the 3-word sets to create new words or phrases. For example: In a set including "smith," "fore," and "game," the added word would be "word" (creating "wordsmith," "foreword," and "word game").

1. Time, dive, shell: _____

2. Train, silver, proof: _bullet_____

3. Head, root, broken: _____

4. Range, air, butt:_____

5. Dance, broad, play: _____

Answers on page 232.

CRYPTOKU

Answer the clues below to fill in the grid and discover the 9 different letters used in each 3 by 3 box. Just like a standard crossword, answers read across and down; numbers in parenthesis indicate how many letters are in the solution. And, like a code-doku, each letter appears only once in each 3 by 3 box. When complete, the shaded squares will reveal a mystery phrase.

I		T	¹H		N	⁶A		S
	K			B			T	
		⁷S			A			I
	E		²A		S		B	
B	³N			H		I		⁸T
	T		⁴		B		A	
		E		S				B
	⁹I		⁵E	¹⁰	T		N	
T		K		N		E		A

ACROSS

1. Female chicken (3)
2. Preposition (2)
3. Egyptian symbol (4)
4. Point of an old pen (3)
5. Devour (3)

DOWN

6. Doctor's command, with "say" (2)
7. Transgression (3)
8. Seventh music note (2)
9. First person, to be (2)
10. Article (2)

Answers on page 232.

PARKING TICKETS

Susan works as a parking enforcement officer in downtown Charlotte. Today she wrote tickets for five illegally-parked cars. Help her sort out her paperwork by matching each ticket to the correct car (model and color), street location, and the time at which it was written.

1. The Toyota was ticketed one hour after the green car.

2. Of the Toyota and the Chevrolet, one was silver and the other was the last to be ticketed.

3. The ticket on Tawny Terrace was written at 12:00pm. Susan wrote the ticket for the silver car sometime before that.

4. The brown car was ticketed 2 hours after the Nissan.

5. Susan wrote the ticket on Sandy Street sometime before the one for the double-parked Chevrolet.

6. The Mazda was ticketed 2 hours after the black car.

7. Susan was on Apple Avenue sometime before 12:30pm.

8. The ticket on Lantern Lane wasn't written at 1:00pm.

		Models					Colors					Locations				
		Chevrolet	Honda	Nissan	Mazda	Toyota	Black	Blue	Brown	Green	Silver	Apple Ave.	Lantern Ln.	Raffle Rd.	Sandy St.	Tawny Terr.
Times	10:00am															
	11:00am															
	12:00pm															
	1:00pm															
	2:00pm															
Locations	Apple Ave.										
	Lantern Ln.										
	Raffle Rd.										
	Sandy St.										
	Tawny Terr.										
Colors	Black					
	Blue					
	Brown					
	Green					
	Silver					

Times	Models	Colors	Locations
10:00am			
11:00am			
12:00pm			
1:00pm			
2:00pm			

Answers on page 232.

THRILLING READS

ACROSS

1. Beauty queen's crown
6. Eskimo boot
12. Map book
13. Seinfeld sidekick Benes
14. 2009 James Patterson thriller
16. Tropical hurricane
17. Heavy weight
18. EMT destinations
19. "Skyfall" singer
21. 1995 James Patterson thriller
25. Maine and Montana, in France
26. Affleck of "Good Will Hunting"
27. Do a checkout chore
28. Short opera solo
32. 2013 James Patterson thriller
35. Soldier's quarters
36. Singer ___ Marie ("Lady T")
37. Final approvals
38. Koko's weapons

DOWN

1. Ambassador's skill
2. Response to "Nice job!"
3. Leaning to one side
4. Most impetuous
5. Puts in like piles
6. "And you can quote ___ that!"
7. Director Grosbard or a curved Alaskan knife
8. Dorothy Gale's state: abbr.
9. Confetti, after a parade
10. Prepare for installation, as a carpet
11. Economist John Maynard
15. Bobby's stick
19. Those seeking junior partners?
20. "Out of Africa" author
21. Skewered chunks
22. Roma's country
23. In a wise way
24. Spain's "Nile"
28. Ballet and bonsai
29. Eucalyptus or sycamore

30. "I Whistle a Happy ___"

31. Santa ___ (desert winds)

33. Good-sized sizes

34. Big boss, briefly

1	2	3	4	5		6	7	8	9	10	11
12						13					
14				15							
16								17			
		18				19	20				
21	22	23			24						
25					26						
27				28				29	30	31	
32		33	34								
35						36					
37						38					

Answers on page 232.

WHAT'S THE CRIME?

The following phrases are all anagrams for a specific white collar crime. What is it?

TRINIDAD SINGER

DAINTIER GRINDS

STRIDING RAINED

DARNING DIRTIES

Answer on page 232.

WHAT'S THE CRIME?

The following phrases are all anagrams for a specific white collar crime. What is it?

ARCADE CRUD DRIFT

ARCTIC DAD FURRED

CIRCA DRAFTER DUD

CRAFTED ARC DRUID

Answer on page 232.

THE GEM THIEF

A company that sold gems found that 5 types of gems had been stolen from their warehouse. There was 1 gem of the first type, 2 of the second type, 3 of the third type, 4 of the fourth type, and 5 of the fifth type. From the information given below, can you tell how many gemstones of each kind were taken?

1. There are more than 2 diamonds.

2. There are fewer than 4 rubies.

3. There are more rubies than pieces of topaz.

4. There is an even number of pearls.

5. There are more sapphires than rubies or pearls, but they are not the most plentiful gem.

Answers on page 233.

TRACK THE FUGITIVE

The investigator is tracking the fugitive's past trips in order to find and recover information that was left behind in five cities. Each city was visited only once. Can you put together the travel timeline, using the information below?

1. Indianapolis was not the third city visited.

2. The fugitive went north along the coastline immediately after visiting Las Vegas.

3. Pensacola was neither the first nor last city visited.

4. Montpelier was visited sometime before Indianapolis, but not immediately before.

5. Portland was visited sometime before Pensacola, but not immediately before.

Answers on page 233.

A FAMOUS ATTEMPT

Cryptograms are messages in substitution code. Break the code to read the message. For example, THE SMART CAT might become FVO QWGDF JGF if F is substituted for T, V for H, O for E, and so on.

LHFBY ACHHTI FBN DHCJSMHI OXFHMBOM

FBN ZCSB FBUXTB MIOFEMN FXOFJHFW

EHTICB TB 1962, QSMB JSMV QMHM FXX TB

JSMTH 30I. QSTXM JSMV FHM DMXTMPMN

JC SFPM NHCQBMN, JSM OFIM SFI BMPMH

DMMB CLLTOTFXXV OXCIMN.

Answer on page 233.

WHODUNIT?

A rebus follows its own type of alphabet: a mixture of letters, symbols, and pictures. Look carefully at the rebus below. You should be able to "read" the solution to the clue in the puzzle's title.

Answer on page 233.

OVERHEARD INFORMATION PART I

Read the story below, then turn the page and answer the questions.

The detective overheard the thief tell her accomplice about the different places where she stashed the loot. She said, "The ruby bracelet and the sapphire ring are both found in the summer house in Claremont Heights. The pearl necklace is hidden in the penthouse suite of the condo building in New York. The vintage wine is in the crawlspace of the farmhouse in Trevalyn. The gold coins are in the safety deposit box in the bank in Potosie."

OVERHEARD INFORMATION PART II

(Do not read this until you have read the previous page!)
The investigator overheard the information about where the stolen loot was stored, but didn't have anywhere to write it down! Answer the questions below to help the investigator remember.

1. Two items are found at the summer house. What are they?

   A. Ruby bracelet and sapphire ring

   B. Ruby ring and sapphire bracelet

   C. Ruby bracelet and pearl necklace

   D. Ruby bracelet and gold coins

2. The pearl necklace is found in this location.

   A. Claremont Heights
   B. New York
   C. Trevalyn
   D. Potosie

3. The vintage wine is found in this part of the farmhouse.

   A. Attic
   B. Basement
   C. Crawlspace
   D. Safe

4. The bank is found in this location.

   A. Claremont Heights
   B. New York
   C. Trevalyn
   D. Potosie

Answers on page 233.

SEEN AT THE SCENE
PART I

Study this picture of the crime scene for 1 minute, then turn the page.

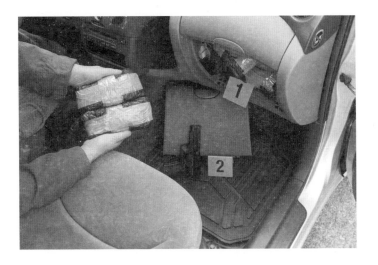

SEEN AT THE SCENE
PART II

(Do not read this until you have read the previous page!)
Which image exactly matches the crime scene?

1.

2.

3.

4.

Answer on page 233.

PICK YOUR POISON

There are five bottles before you, but they've gotten jumbled up. Poison is found in one of them. If you arrange them from left to right, following the instructions given below, you will be able to know where the poison is found.

1. The blue bottle is to the right of the purple bottle, but not immediately to the right.

2. The yellow bottle is not next to the purple bottle.

3. The brown bottle and the white bottle are next to each other.

4. The white bottle is next to the yellow bottle.

5. The poison is found in the bottle that is the second from the left.

Answer on page 234.

DNA SEQUENCE

Examine the two images below carefully. Are these sequences a match or not?

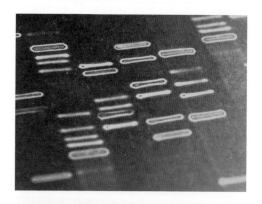

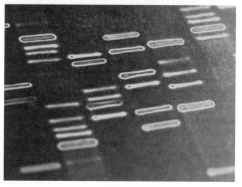

Answer on page 234.

THE SUSPECT FLED TO...

The letters in the country QATAR can be found in boxes 5, 8, 10, and 16, but not necessarily in that order. Similarly, the letters in all the other country names below can be found in the boxes indicated. Insert all the letters of the alphabet into the boxes; if you do this correctly, the shaded cells will reveal another nation.

Hint: Look for names that share a single letter.

BELGIUM: 1, 4, 7, 9, 18, 23, 24

CHILE: 4, 7, 9, 13, 21

DENMARK: 7, 8, 10, 11, 12, 17, 24

FRANCE: 7, 8, 10, 11, 21, 26

GERMANY: 1, 7, 8, 10, 11, 15, 24

HOLLAND: 9, 10, 11, 12, 13, 25

JAPAN: 10, 11, 14, 19

KUWAIT: 3, 4, 5, 10, 17, 18

LATVIA: 4, 5, 9, 10, 22

MEXICO: 4, 7, 20, 21, 24, 25

PERU: 7, 8, 14, 18

QATAR: 5, 8, 10, 16

SWEDEN: 2, 3, 7, 11, 12

ZIMBABWE: 3, 4, 6, 7, 10, 23, 24

1	2	3	4	5	6	7	8	9	10	11	12	13

14	15	16	17	18	19	20	21	22	23	24	25	26

Answers on page 234.

SPY SCRAMBLE

You're tracking down a mole. You know when he's meeting with his contact to relay information, but you don't know where. However, you've found a list of random words that you think might combine to form an anagram of the location. Can you unscramble the letters and find the meetup details?

OF REST REP VERSE LIME MAKER RENT

Answer on page 234.

MOTEL HIDEOUT

A thief hides out in one of the 45 motel rooms listed in the chart below. The motel's in-house detective received a sheet of four clues, signed "The Logical Thief."

1. The first digit is a prime number.

2. Both digits are even.

3. The second digit cannot be divided by 3.

4. The second digit is not larger than the first digit.

51	52	53	54	55	56	57	58	59
41	42	43	44	45	46	47	48	49
31	32	33	34	35	36	37	38	39
21	22	23	24	25	26	27	28	29
11	12	13	14	15	16	17	18	19

Answer on page 234.

STOLEN ART

Each piece of artwork listed below has been stolen, and only some have been recovered. Every piece of artwork listed is contained within the group of letters. Words can be found in a straight line horizontally, vertically, or diagonally. They may be read either forward or backward.

CHEZ TORTONI (Édouard Manet)

THE CONCERT (Johannes Vermeer)

FEMME ASSISE (Henri Matisse)

LANDSCAPE WITH COTTAGES (Rembrandt van Rijn)

MONA LISA (Leonardo da Vinci)

LE PIGEON AUX PETITS POIS (Pablo Picasso)

PORTRAIT OF A LADY (Gustav Klimt)

POPPY FLOWERS (Vincent van Gogh)

SAINT JEROME WRITING (Caravaggio)

THE SCREAM (Edvard Munch)

SELF-PORTRAIT (Rembrandt van Rijn)

WATERLOO BRIDGE, LONDON (Claude Monet)

```
P  S  U  F  S  S  G  L  P  B  R  F  E  B  D  B  L  T  Z  P  W
T  I  I  M  A  E  W  G  Z  J  Y  S  R  F  K  M  N  V  D  A  W
N  O  P  N  Z  G  A  Q  K  R  X  E  H  G  A  V  A  F  B  R  V
N  P  S  N  O  A  T  P  J  M  H  H  X  E  V  O  E  J  R  A  P
E  S  A  O  K  T  E  C  D  Q  D  G  R  I  H  Q  W  P  S  Y  K
P  T  I  N  C  T  R  T  Q  K  R  C  W  I  E  G  O  I  Y  Y  S
O  I  N  P  P  O  L  O  J  W  S  Z  U  L  W  D  L  J  Q  R  S
R  T  T  L  C  C  O  J  T  E  D  D  W  O  T  A  Y  F  E  H  E
T  E  J  X  L  H  O  A  H  Z  F  B  Q  M  N  V  O  W  N  I  L
R  P  E  K  Y  T  B  T  O  T  E  E  Y  O  Y  U  O  V  T  Q  F
A  X  R  E  H  I  R  T  C  S  M  H  M  G  G  L  K  R  Y  X  P
I  U  O  C  A  W  I  K  P  U  Y  L  C  M  F  E  E  I  B  X  O
T  A  M  S  K  E  D  C  N  A  I  F  U  Y  E  C  N  X  D  G  R
O  N  E  D  M  P  G  X  X  R  E  A  P  C  N  A  W  T  G  H  T
F  O  W  N  T  A  E  Z  Q  T  F  P  P  O  Y  L  S  K  Y  V  R
A  E  R  M  D  C  L  P  Y  E  O  Q  C  R  R  A  R  S  W  L  A
L  G  I  A  E  S  O  Z  T  P  I  E  T  E  X  Q  C  G  I  B  I
A  I  T  A  I  D  N  X  D  Z  H  F  J  J  S  F  Z  W  W  S  T
D  P  I  B  A  N  D  N  F  T  G  U  Q  C  Y  B  V  R  O  W  E
Y  E  N  P  Y  A  O  Q  L  I  K  S  G  R  B  P  K  O  K  C  B
H  L  G  E  A  L  N  V  S  B  H  H  T  Z  Z  Z  Q  H  J  C  A
```

Answers on page 234.

INTERCEPTION

You've intercepted a message between a criminal who fled and his accomplice. But the message doesn't seem to make sense! Can you discover the criminal's current location hidden in the message?

CAN HE ARRANGE RED LIGHT OR TWO TIMES

ELECTRICITY,

NEXT CENTURY?

Answer on page 235.

WHAT DO YOU SEE?
PART I

Study this picture of the crime scene for 1 minute, then turn the page.

WHAT DO YOU SEE? PART II

(Do not read this until you have read the previous page!)
Which image exactly matches the crime scene?

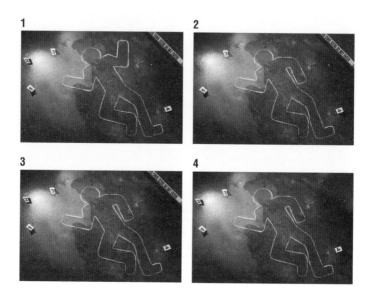

1

2

3

4

Answer on page 235.

NO BONES ABOUT IT

A typical adult human skeleton consists of 206 bones.
Pick out the fake bone from each list.

1. Wrist bones:
   A. trapezium
   B. trapezoid
   C. capitate
   D. rhomboid

2. Finger bones, or phalanges:
   A. proximal
   B. intermediate
   C. pointal
   D. distal

3. Leg bones:
   A. femur
   B. paella
   C. patella
   D. fibula

4. Ankle bones:
   A. calcaneus
   B. talus
   C. perpendicular
   D. navicular

5. Ankle bones:
   A. proximal
   B. intermediate
   C. distal
   D. porkal

6. Vertebrae:
   A. vertical
   B. cervical
   C. lumbar
   D. thoracic

7. Facial bones:
   A. mandible
   B. nasal
   C. palatine
   D. pimpal

8. Skull:
   A. temporal
   B. capital
   C. occipital
   D. frontal

Answers on page 235.

KEEPING THE PEACE

A rebus follows its own type of alphabet: a mixture of letters, symbols, and pictures. Look carefully at the rebus below. You should be able to "read" the solution to the clue in the puzzle's title.

Answer on page 235.

FIND THE WITNESS

On Mitchell Street, there are 5 houses that are identical to each other. You need to gather a witness statement from Michelle and Trevor Banks, but without any address on the doors you are not sure which house to approach. You know that the Banks have two teenaged sons. The staff at the coffee shop around the corner and your own observations give you some clues. From the information given, can you find the right house?

a. There are kids at three of the houses.

b. The single dad lives between the vacant house and the bachelor.

c. The single mom likes the big lot she has at the last corner house.

d. The vacant house is not on the corner.

House A   House B   House C   House D   House E

Answer on page 235.

POLICE DISPATCHER

Trevor was on-call today as the Libertyville Police Department's primary dispatcher. He received six calls during the morning shift, each from a different part of town, and each for a different reason. He dispatched a different officer for each of these six calls. Using only the clues below, help him sort out his dispatch log by matching each call to its time, location, and assigned officer.

1. Of Brenda and whoever was dispatched to deal with the alarm, one went Downtown and the other was sent to the North End.

2. Harry didn't leave at 11:45am.

3. One officer was dispatched to the scene of a truck accident 3 hours after the call to go Downtown.

4. Jeffrey was sent out sometime after the Midtown call.

5. Of Neville and whoever went to investigate the stolen car, one was dispatched at 10:15am and the other went to Midtown.

6. One officer (who wasn't Linda) was sent to check on a cat stuck in a tree 45 minutes before another was sent to the North End.

7. The 10:15am call, Harry's call, the one for the South End, and the one for the bank robbery involved four different officers.

8. Brenda headed out sometime after whoever went Uptown. The Uptown dispatch didn't happen at either 8:45am or 10:15am.

9. The officer that went to the South End left 2 hours and 15 minutes after whoever went to the scene of the bank robbery.

10. Neither Dale nor Linda was dispatched to investigate the trespassing call.

		Officers						Calls						Locations					
		Brenda	Dale	Harry	Jeffrey	Linda	Neville	Accident	Alarm	Bank robbery	Cat in tree	Stolen car	Trespassing	Bus. District	Downtown	Midtown	North End	South End	Uptown
Times	8:45am																		
	9:30am																		
	10:15am																		
	11:00am																		
	11:45am																		
	12:30pm																		
Locations	Bus. District																		
	Downtown																		
	Midtown																		
	North End																		
	South End																		
	Uptown																		
Calls	Accident																		
	Alarm																		
	Bank robbery																		
	Cat in tree																		
	Stolen car																		
	Trespassing																		

Times	Officers	Calls	Locations
8:45am			
9:30am			
10:15am			
11:00am			
11:45am			
12:30pm			

Answers on page 235.

CRIME ON TV

ACROSS

1. Aptly named forensics crime show on Fox
6. Milkmaid's needs
11. Byron or Keats
12. In ____ (agitated)
13. City visited by pilgrims
14. Beauty pageant crown
15. Ailing chemistry teacher turns to crime (AMC)
17. Leonardo ____, a.k.a. Fibonacci
18. They tempted Ulysses
21. "Bravo, torero!"
24. Captain in "The Caine Mutiny"
25. Cool red giant in the sky
27. Range of sizes, briefly
28. Donny or Marie, by birth
29. "8 Mile" rapper
32. Dark yet funny TBS mystery starring Alia Shawkat
37. "Who's there?" reply, perhaps

38. Bolivian city, former capital
39. Oscar actress Garson
40. Go ballistic, with "out"
41. Avian abodes
42. Dark-comedy crime drama with Billy Bob Thornton as a hitman in Minnesota (FX)

DOWN

1. Big flop
2. German/Czech river
3. "Good work!"
4. Object of a manhunt
5. Supporting, as tomato plants
6. City on the Ganges (or Lord Jim's ship)
7. Not ____ of (no trace of)
8. Where diner patrons may prefer to sit
9. Former Italian money
10. End of many Dutch town names

16. NASA orbiter
18. Four-sided figs.
19. Chemical suffix
20. Puts out, as a record
22. Anaheim baseball team, in box scores
23. Fish-catching eagle
25. Debark
26. John O'Hara's "Appointment in ___"

28. The Wildcats of the NCAA, for short
30. Shea Stadium mascot
31. Cake decorators
32. Communicate by hand
33. Being, in Paris
34. One who's sorry
35. "King Lear" or "Hamlet": Abbr.
36. Lennon's wife

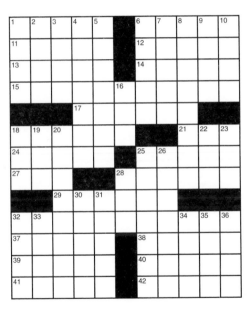

Answers on page 236.

THE GEM THIEF

A company that sold gems found that 5 types of gems had been stolen from their warehouse. There was 1 gem of the first type, 2 of the second type, 3 of the third type, 4 of the fourth type, and 5 of the fifth type. From the information given below, can you tell how many gemstones of each kind were taken?

1. There are odd numbers of pearls and peridots.

2. There are at least 3 pieces of aquamarine.

3. There are more pieces of jade than emeralds.

4. There are fewer aquamarines than pearls.

5. There are fewer emeralds than aquamarines, but more emeralds than peridots.

6. There are two more pearls than pieces of jade.

Answers on page 236.

PICK YOUR POISON

There are four bottles before you, but they've gotten jumbled up. Poison is found in one of them. If you arrange them from left to right, following the instructions given below, you will be able to know where the poison is found.

1. Two bottles are red, and they are not next to each other.

2. The pink bottle is either the second bottle from the left or the bottle at the far right.

3. The poison is in the bottle between the two bottles of the same color.

4. The pink bottle is not next to the bottle with the poison nor does it contain the poison.

5. The orange bottle is not next to the pink bottle.

Answers on page 236.

A SUCCESSFUL DISAPPEARANCE

Cryptograms are messages in substitution code. Break the code to read the message. For example, THE SMART CAT might become FVO QWGDF JGF if F is substituted for T, V for H, O for E, and so on.

ZEZTGIM ATMFTG, CIMG BG BIUT,

RBOTKKZTMZR TP PJZ TNZ IH 39. BG 1933,

ATMFTG, JZM CIWHMBZGR, TGR TGIPJZM

FTG PMBZR PI MIC T YEIPJBGN OPIMZ.

ATMFTG'O TYYIFKEBYZ OJIP PJZ

OPIMZ IUGZM.

ATMFTG OZMSZR OZSZG WZTMO BG

KMBOIG CZHIMZ OJZ ZOYTKZR PI OZZ JZM

HTFBEW. HMIF PJZMZ OJZ RBOTKKZTMZR,

YIFFQGBYTPBGN UBPJ JZM HTFBEW SBT

GZUOKTKZM TRO.

Answer on page 236.

DNA SEQUENCE

Examine the two images below carefully. Are these sequences a match or not?

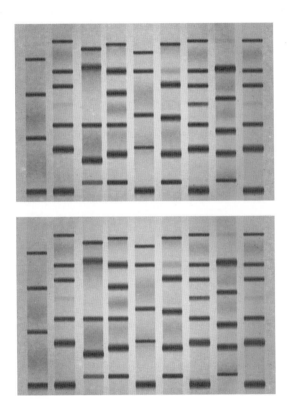

Answer on page 237.

TO THE LETTER

Fill in the blanks with words that are nearly identical to each other. Figure out the first word, then drop one letter to discover the second word. Do not rearrange the letters.

It may be dangerous to _____ a person who

snatches your _____.

Persue , purse

Answers on page 237.

CROSSED WORDS

Unscramble the words in each line to solve the puzzle. The words cross on a letter that they share.

```
        R
        C
        T
  E E V R S
        P
        O
```
protect ,serve

Answers on page 237.

MOTEL HIDEOUT

A thief hides out in one of the 45 motel rooms listed in the chart below. The motel's in-house detective received a sheet of four clues, signed "The Logical Thief." Using these clues, the detective found the room number within 15 minutes—but by that time, the thief had fled. Can you find the thief's motel room more quickly?

1. The number is even.

2. The sum of the digits is odd.

3. Either the number 4 is one of the digits or the number is divisible by 4, but not both.

4. The sum of the digits is greater than 10.

51	52	53	54	55	56	57	58	59
41	42	43	44	45	46	47	48	49
31	32	33	34	35	36	37	38	39
21	22	23	24	25	26	27	28	29
11	12	13	14	15	16	17	18	19

Answer on page 237.

POISON!
PART I

Long a favorite of mystery-novel writers and opportunistic bad guys, poison has an ancient and infamous reputation. Read some facts about poison below, then turn the page.

Deadly Nightshade, aka belladonna: Every part of this herb is poisonous, but the berries are most dangerous. The poison attacks the nervous system instantly, causing a rapid pulse, hallucinations, convulsions, ataxia (lack of muscle coordination) and coma.

Wolfsbane: This deadly plant was used as an arrow poison by the ancient Chinese, and its name comes from the Greek word meaning "dart." Wolfsbane takes a while to work, but when it does, it causes extreme anxiety, chest pain, and death from respiratory arrest.

Hemlock: This plant is probably the best known of the herbaceous poisons: It was used to knock off the Greek philosopher Socrates. Hemlock is poisonous down to the last leaf and will often send you into a coma before it finishes you for good.

Arsenic—colorless, tasteless, and odorless—has been called "the poison of kings" because for hundreds of years it was the poison of choice used by members of the ruling class to murder one another.

This close relative of phosphorous exists in a variety of compounds, not all of which are poisonous. Women in Victorian times used to rub a diluted arsenic compound into their skin to improve their complexions, and some modern medications used to treat cancer actually contain arsenic. When certain arsenic compounds are concentrated, however, they're deadly; arsenic has been blamed for widespread death through groundwater contamination.

There are five ways a person can be exposed to poison: ingestion (through the mouth), inhalation (breathed in through the nose or mouth), ocular (in the eyes), dermal (on the skin), and parenteral (from bites or stings).

POISON!
PART II

(Do not read this until you have read the previous page!)

1. Arsenic is a green powder.

   ____ True

   _✔_ False

2. Parenteral exposure means that poison seeped through the skin.

   ____ True

   _✔_ False

3. The berries of nightshade are poisonous, but not the leaves.

   ____ True

   _✔_ False

4. Socrates was killed by hemlock.

   _✔_ True

   ____ False

5. Wolfsbane does not work immediately.

   _✔_ True

   ____ False

Answers on page 237.

SEEN AT THE SCENE
PART I

Study this picture of the crime scene for 1 minute, then turn the page.

SEEN AT THE SCENE
PART II

(Do not read this until you have read the previous page!)
Which image exactly matches the crime scene?

1.

2.

3.

4.

Answer on page 237.

CRIME ANAGRAMS

Unscramble each word or phrase below to reveal a word or phrase related to criminal charges.

BIRD TUITIONS

COALITIONIST

AS VEXATION

LAVA MINDS

PLOT FISHING

MASHER TANS

GALS KNIT

A WEIRD FUR

Answers on page 237.

TRACK THE FUGITIVE

The investigator is tracking the fugitive's past trips in order to find and recover information that was left behind in five cities. Each city was visited only once. Can you put together the travel timeline, using the information below?

1. From Berlin, the fugitive went directly to the other capital city in Europe.

2. Tokyo was not the last city visited.

3. Santiago was visited sometime before, but not immediately before, Lisbon.

4. Algiers was one of the first three cities visited, but not the first.

5. From Asia, the fugitive went directly to South America.

Answers on page 237.

FINGERPRINT MATCH

Find the matching fingerprint(s). There may be more than one.

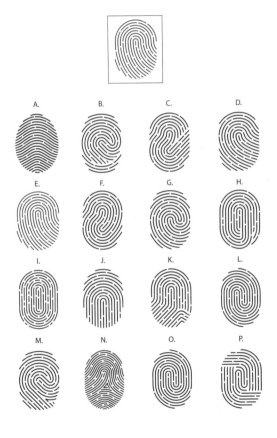

Answer on page 237.

IN SEARCH OF EVIDENCE

ACROSS

1. Scottish Gaelic language
5. Kaiser or Maxwell
8. Inflammatory suffix
12. Prison's antithesis, with "the"
14. Fire and fury
15. One of the lab techniques in 26-Across
16. On the authority of
17. Light tan
18. Acqua Di ___ (Armani fragrance)
19. "I'll take that as ___"
20. Piece of copper
21. Highway sign
22. Two-colored ermine
24. CPR giver, perhaps
26. Field of "CSI"
31. "Illmatic" rapper
32. Not those
34. Titled woman
36. Queen of the Nile
39. Start of an Irish flier
40. British rec. giant

41. Rowing gear
42. Digital camera variety, for short
43. Ink impressions that reveal responsibility
46. Boy or girl lead-in
47. Time to vote
48. Critical evaluation
49. Velocity: abbr.
50. Composer of "Dido and Aeneas"

DOWN

2. Rat or squirrel
3. Car option that slides open
4. Terminal datum
5. She turned men to pigs in "The Odyssey"
6. Add decorations
7. Proves false
8. Not online, briefly
9. Evergreen forest of subarctic lands
10. Start to burn
11. Desert lilies

13. Prism bands

16. Que ___? ("What's going on?")

21. Draw on glass

23. Classy

25. Cell division

27. Former Ford compacts

28. Another name for starfish

29. Hawaii, before 1959: abbr.

30. Heavy silk fabric

33. Generator element

34. Render lean

35. After-dinner freebies

37. Receive with enthusiasm

38. Did the wrong thing

44. Pistol, in old gangster movies

45. Contract to protect trade secrets: abbr.

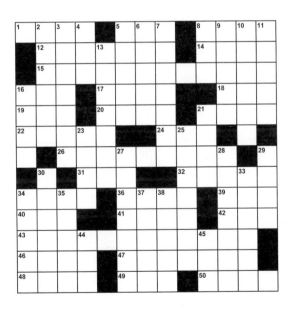

Answers on page 238.

CRYPTO-LOGIC

Each of the numbers in the sequence below represents a letter. Use the mathematical clues to determine which number stands for which letter and reveal the encrypted word.

Hint: Remember that a / indicates divided by, and that all sums in parentheses must be done first.

15398256

CLUES:

R repeats
R - (R - 1) = T
2T = E
E x R = S
S + E = L
L / 2 = Y
3 x (1/2Y) = C
(C-R) x 2 = K
1/2K - T = I

Answer on page 238.

OVERHEARD INFORMATION PART I

Read the story below, then turn the page and answer the questions.

The detective overheard the jewelry thief tell his accomplice about the different places where he stashed the loot. He said, "The pearls are inside the egg carton in the fridge. The opals are in the ice cube tray in the freezer. The rubies are in the cereal box. The garnets are in the medicine cabinet in the upstairs bathroom."

OVERHEARD INFORMATION PART II

(Do not read this until you have read the previous page!)
The investigator overheard the information about where the stolen loot was stored, but didn't have anywhere to write it down! Answer the questions below to help the investigator remember.

1. The garnets are found in this room.

    A. Kitchen

    B. Upstairs bathroom

    C. Downstairs bathroom

    D. We are not told.

2. The pearls are found in this location.

    A. Refrigerator

    B. Freezer

    C. Kitchen cabinet

    D. Medicine cabinet

3. What is found in the ice cube tray?

    A. Pearls

    B. Opals

    C. Rubies

    D. Garnets

4. What is found in the cereal box?

    A. Pearls

    B. Opals

    C. Rubies

    D. Garnets

Answers on page 238.

WILL THE PERP GO TO JAIL?

Change just one letter on each line to go from the top word to the bottom word. Do not change the order of the letters. You must have a common English word at each step.

PERP

_____

_____

_____ get ready for a trip

_____

_____

_____

_____

JAIL

Answers on page 238.

THE GEM THIEF

A company that sold gems found that 5 types of gems had been stolen from their warehouse. There was 1 gem of the first type, 2 of the second type, 3 of the third type, 4 of the fourth type, and 5 of the fifth type. From the information given below, can you tell how many gemstones of each kind were taken?

1. There are two fewer rubies than garnets.

2. Opals are neither the most nor least plentiful gem.

3. There are more opals than diamonds.

4. There is an even number of emeralds.

5. There are more opals than rubies.

Answers on page 238.

You've intercepted a message between a criminal who fled and his accomplice. But the message doesn't seem to make sense! Can you discover a piece of hidden information in the message?

MOM WE SEE IT

THEM TOO THEN DANCED EXTRA SILLY

FEAR TO GOING SEE KIDNAPPER BOSS

VIP AREA NEAR PADLOCK

Answer on page 238.

CRYPTO-LOGIC

Each of the numbers in the sequence below represents a letter. Use the mathematical clues to determine which number stands for which letter and reveal the encrypted word.

Hint: Remember that a / indicates divided by, and that all sums in parentheses must be done first.

7 3 5 3 9 6 2 8 3

CLUES:

The value equal to the number of times it is present represents E

T squared is 12E

I squared + I = T

P - S = V

V = 2 X I squared

S X P = P

D + C = P + E

D > T

Answer on page 239.

FOND OF ROBBING BANKS

Cryptograms are messages in substitution code. Break the code to read the message. For example, THE SMART CAT might become FVO QWGDF JGF if F is substituted for T, V for H, O for E, and so on.

C GCFB LHGGRL HM PYR 1940O CFJ 1950O,

MLRJRLZNB WLCFP JQFF TCO NCDDRJ

"PYR EHJRLF AHYF JZDDZFWRL." CMPRL

CF RONCIR MLHE NQOPHJV ZF 1958, YR TCO

CJJRJ PH PYR EHOP TCFPRJ DZOP. YR TCO

MHQFJ JRCJ MLHE NCQORO QFBFHTF

ZF 1959.

Answer on page 239.

THE JUDGE

Judge Penrose ruled on five criminal cases today at the Twelfth Circuit Court. Each case involved a different crime, and none of the five defendants received the same sentence or had the same lawyer. Using only the clues below, determine each defendant's crime and length of sentence (in months), as well as the name of their lawyer.

1. Coretta Colson represented either Rachel or the person convicted of assault.

2. The shoplifter received a longer sentence than Rachel.

3. The perjurer's sentence was twice as long as the one handed down to Bill Barrett's client.

4. Of Nelson and the perjurer, one was represented by Orietta Oswald. The other got an 8-month sentence.

5. Whoever was convicted of identity theft received a sentence that was twice as long as Rachel's.

6. Bill Barrett's client, the person who received the 8-month sentence and Annabelle were three different people.

7. Frederick's sentence was twice as long as that of the person convicted of grand theft.

8. Annabelle was sentenced to 4 months in Wallace County Prison.

9. Nelson's case had nothing to with assault charges.

10. Coretta Colson's client wasn't convicted of grand theft, and Martin McFerry's client wasn't the shoplifter.

		Defendants					Crimes					Lawyers				
		Annabelle	Frederick	Jasmine	Nelson	Rachel	assault	grand theft	ID theft	perjury	shoplifting	Barrett	Colson	McFerry	Oswald	Zimmerman
Sentences	1 month															
	2 months															
	4 months															
	8 months															
	16 months															
Lawyers	Barrett															
	Colson															
	McFerry															
	Oswald															
	Zimmerman															
Crimes	assault															
	grand theft															
	ID theft															
	perjury															
	shoplifting															

Sentences	Defendants	Crimes	Lawyers
1 month			
2 months			
4 months			
8 months			
16 months			

Answers on page 239.

THE "MOST HATED MAN IN THE WORLD"

In 1932, the kidnapping of Charles Lindbergh, Jr., son of the famous aviator and his wife Anne, shocked the nation. Although a ransom was paid, the child was murdered. Bruno Richard Hauptmann was accused and convicted of the crime. Every word listed is contained within the group of letters. Words can be found in a straight line horizontally, vertically, or diagonally. They may be read either forward or backward.

ABDUCTION

ANNE MORROW

CARPENTER

CHARLES

CRIME OF THE CENTURY

GOLD CERTIFICATE

ELECTRIC CHAIR

EXECUTION

JOHN CONDON

KIDNAPPING

LADDER

LINDBERGH

RANSOM NOTE

RICHARD HAUPTMANN

```
E C G Y Q J P J G N I E B N E R D
S R J K H Q V R S H V R R N T E Y
D I U I D N X K X K O A C A A D K
Y M X J F G M F I W N N E M C D K
R E T N E P R A C S A O K T I A E
G O T Z G U H U O B D D D P F L L
N F I S N R U M D N E N A U I J E
I T G E X E N U I K J O N A T C C
P H Q X Z O C Y N M A C N H R X T
P E P K T T H B O J Q N E D E B R
A C J E I C A H I V X H M R C M I
N E T O X Y R V T B H O O A D O C
D N N R V E L W U H J J R H L K C
I T L I H R E D C Z R J R C O G H
K U V J U V S A E Q Q O O I G F A
N R M N U N B U X W H Y W R M T I
T Y C A R H G R E B D N I L X Z R
```

Answers on page 239.

THE BODY FARM
PART I

Read the following information about the University of Tennessee's Body Farm, then turn the page.

Forensic anthropologist William M. Bass had a dream. As an expert in the field of human decomposition, he couldn't fathom why a facility devoted to this under-studied process didn't exist. So, in 1972, working in conjunction with the University of Tennessee, he founded the Body Farm or, more specifically, the University of Tennessee Forensic Anthropology Facility.

Just outside of Knoxville, the eerie three-acre wooded plot that Bass claimed for his scientific studies—which is surrounded by a razor wire fence—is where an unspecified number of cadavers in various states of decomposition are kept. While some hang out completely in the open, others spend their time in shallow graves or entombed in vaults. Others dip their toes and other body parts in ponds. And a few spend eternity inside sealed car trunks.

So why is this done? What can be learned from observing human flesh and bone decay in the hot Tennessee sun? Plenty, according to scientists and members of the media who have studied the Body Farm. "Nearly everything known about the science of human decomposition comes from one place—forensic anthropologist William Bass'

Body Farm," declared CNN in high praise of the facility. The bodies are strewn in different positions and under varying circumstances for reasons far from happenstance. Each cadaver will display differing reactions to decomposition, insect and wildlife interference, and the elements. These invaluable indicators can help investigators zero-in on the cause and time of death in current and future criminal cases.

Bass himself claims that knowledge gleaned from Body Farm studies has proven especially helpful to murder investigations. "People will have alibis for certain time periods, and if you can determine death happened at another time, it makes a difference in the court case," said Bass. Even the prestigious FBI uses the Body Farm as a real-world simulator to help train its agents. Every February, representatives visit the site to dig for bodies that farm hands have prepared as simulated crime scenes. "We have five of them down there for them," explains Bass. "They excavate the burials and look for evidence that we put there."

Since the inception of Bass's original Body Farm, other facilities have been established, including one at Western Carolina University. Ideally, Bass would like to see body farms all over the nation. Since decaying bodies react differently depending on their climate and surroundings, says Bass, "It's important to gather information from other research facilities across the United States."

THE BODY FARM
PART II

(Do not read this until you have read the previous page!)

1. The Body Farm is the only facility of its kind in the United States.

    ____ True

    ____ False

2. One thing studied at the Body Farm is how insects can affect decomposition of cadavers.

    ____ True

    ____ False

3. The Body Farm is a training site for investigators.

    ____ True

    ____ False

4. Climate can greatly affect decomposition rates.

    ____ True

    ____ False

5. The Body Farm was founded in 1942.

    ____ True

    ____ False

Answers on page 239.

SEEN AT THE SCENE PART I

Study this picture of the crime scene for 1 minute, then turn the page.

SEEN AT THE SCENE PART II

(Do not read this until you have read the previous page!)

Which image exactly matches the crime scene?

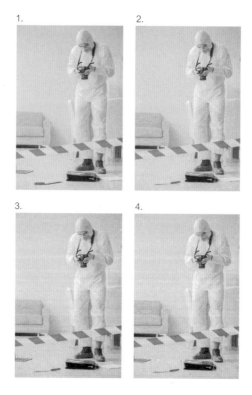

1.

2.

3.

4.

Answer on page 239.

MOTEL HIDEOUT

A thief hides out in one of the 45 motel rooms listed in the chart below. The motel's in-house detective received a sheet of four clues, signed "The Logical Thief." Using these clues, the detective found the room number within 15 minutes—but by that time, the thief had fled. Can you find the thief's motel room more quickly?

1. Each digit is greater than 2.

2. The number is not divisible by 4.

3. If you subtract one digit from the other, the result will be 2, 3, or 4.

4. The first digit is larger than the second.

51	52	53	54	55	56	57	58	59
41	42	43	44	45	46	47	48	49
31	32	33	34	35	36	37	38	39
21	22	23	24	25	26	27	28	29
11	12	13	14	15	16	17	18	19

Answer on page 240.

FBI QUIZ

How much do you know about the FBI?

1. In what year was the Bureau of Investigation, the FBI's predecessor, established?

   A. 1789

   B. 1877

   C. 1908

   D. 1952

2. In what year did the FBI gain its current name?

   A. 1901

   B. 1929

   C. 1935

   D. 1952

3. During what span of years did J. Edgar Hoover lead the FBI and its predecessor organizations?

   A. 1899–1932

   B. 1924–1957

   C. 1941–1979

   D. 1924–1972

4. The training facility in Quantico opened in this year.

   A. 1908

   B. 1932

   C. 1972

   D. 1984

Answers on page 240.

TRACK THE FUGITIVE

The investigator is tracking the fugitive's past trips in order to find and recover information that was left behind in five cities. Each city was visited only once. Can you put together the travel timeline, using the information below?

1. Madrid and Warsaw were visited back to back, not necessarily in that order.

2. Riga was visited before Zagreb, with exactly one other stop in between.

3. Oslo was either the second or third stop.

4. Warsaw was not the final stop.

Answers on page 240.

THE SHOPLIFTER

Wilbur Jones was arrested this evening on multiple shoplifting charges. He's claiming he's innocent, but there's ample video evidence to make the charges stick. Help the police build their case against him by determining the exact details of his five most recent thefts, each of which took place in a different location and on a different day.

1. Of the jacket and the bracelet, one was stolen on Thursday and the other went missing from a shop on Underhill Road.

2. The five thefts were the one on Sunday, the two at Totopia and Greentail, the jacket, and the incident on Prince Avenue.

3. Of Sunday's theft and the one at Dellmans Department Store, one took place on First Street and the other involved a sapphire bracelet.

4. The incident at Nell Headquarters took place one day before the theft on Underhill Road.

5. Of the Totopia theft and the one that took place on Tuesday, one involved a bottle of French cologne and the other happened on Little Lane.

6. D Street was completely shut down on Wednesday due to a water main break, so we know for sure that no thefts occurred there on that day.

7. The sunglasses weren't stolen from a shop on First Street.

		bracelet	cologne	drill	jacket	sunglasses	City Shop	Dellmans	Greentail	Nell HQ	Totopia	D St.	First St.	Little Ln.	Prince Ave.	Underhill Rd.
		Items					**Stores**					**Locations**				
Days	Sunday															
	Monday															
	Tuesday															
	Wednesday															
	Thursday															
Locations	D St.															
	First St.															
	Little Ln.															
	Prince Ave.															
	Underhill Rd.															
Stores	City Shop															
	Dellmans															
	Greentail															
	Nell HQ															
	Totopia															

Days	Items	Stores	Locations
Sunday			
Monday			
Tuesday			
Wednesday			
Thursday			

Answers on page 240.

EITHER/OR

Complete the sentence with two words that are anagrams of each other (e.g. CARE and RACE).

The characters in "Ocean's 11" pulled off a _____ (2 words) partly because they were so _____.

Answers on page 240.

EITHER/OR

Complete the sentence with two words that are anagrams of each other (e.g. CARE and RACE).

The worst shoplifters are those with the _____ need to _____.

Answers on page 240.

DNA SEQUENCE

Examine the two images below carefully. Are these sequences a match or not?

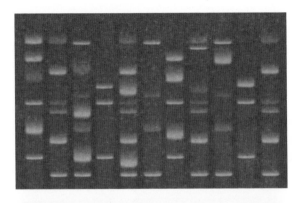

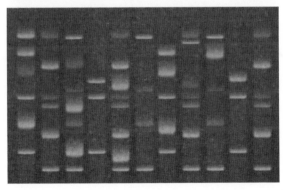

Answer on page 240.

THE CASE OF THE DISAPPEARING GEMS

The letters in ONYX can be found in boxes 6, 13, 19 and 22, but not necessarily in that order. Similarly, the letters in all the other valuables can be found in the boxes indicated. Your task is to insert all the letters of the alphabet into the boxes. If you do this correctly, the shaded cells will reveal two gem stones.

AQUAMARINE: 2, 4, 6, 7, 10, 11, 14, 25

BERYL: 4, 10, 12, 13, 17

CORAL: 2, 5, 10, 17, 22

EMERALD: 2, 3, 4, 10, 14, 17

FIRE OPAL: 2, 4, 10, 17, 20, 22, 23, 25

GARNET: 2, 4, 6, 10, 16, 18

IVORY: 9, 10, 13, 22, 25

JASPER: 1, 2, 4, 10, 21, 23

JEWELS: 1, 4, 17, 21, 26

KUNZITE: 4, 6, 8, 11, 15, 16, 25

ONYX: 6, 13, 19, 22

SAPPHIRE: 2, 4, 10, 21, 23, 24, 25

TOPAZ: 2, 15, 16, 22, 23

1	2	3	4	5	6	7	8	9	10	11	12	13

14	15	16	17	18	19	20	21	22	23	24	25	26

Answers on page 240.

WHAT CHANGED?
PART I

The private detective was at a house party. What did she see in the kitchen? Examine the objects, then turn the page.

WHAT CHANGED?
PART II

Someone was found unconscious at the house party! They said they'd spotted an intruder and then everything went dark. The private detective immediately spotted that one object changed position, and that object was found to be the hastily cleaned weapon. From memory, can you work out what changed position?

Answer on page 240.

MURDER IN NEW ORLEANS

Cryptograms are messages in substitution code. Break the code to read the message. For example, THE SMART CAT might become FVO QWGDF JGF if F is substituted for T, V for H, O for E, and so on.

AH 1918 FHT 1919, F GFH VAQB FH FWY

QYOOIOAZYT HYV IOEYFHP VAQB BAP

GROTYOP AH QBY AQFEAFH-FGYOAUFH

UIGGRHAQX. BAP GROTYO PKOYY PQIKKYT

FNORKQEX, EYFSAHM QBY UFPY RHPIESYT

JIOYSYO.

Answer on page 241.

MASTER OF MYSTERY

ACROSS

1. Checked items
6. Fund-raising lottery
12. Pester, puppy-style
13. More guarded
14. Agatha Christie novel with witches and black magic
16. European blackbirds
17. "The Untouchables" lawman
18. Clever comeback
21. Bygone dignitaries
24. Baggage porter
28. Agatha Christie novel whose title refers to a nursery rhyme
31. Meat cooked and preserved in its own fat
32. Big artery
33. Unlawful takings
34. Short recess

DOWN

1. Prefix meaning "cell"
2. "Hawaii Five-0" island
3. Friends of Tarzan
4. Declines little by little
5. Hardly fresh
6. "Self-Reliance" essayist's monogram
7. "This feels nice!"
8. Main entrance
9. Dragon's breath
10. It's more in an adage
11. You are, in Mexico
15. D-Day assault craft
19. California's Fort ___
20. Back-to-health program, briefly
21. No. on a bill
22. "Rhoda" cast regular David
23. First-rate
25. Medical researcher's goal
26. "The Thin Man" dog
27. Mont Blanc is France's highest
29. First aid box
30. Aliens, for short

Answers on page 241.

PICK YOUR POISON

There are five bottles before you, but they've gotten jumbled up. Poison is found in one of them. If you arrange them from left to right, following the instructions given below, you will be able to know where the poison is found.

1. The teal bottle is to the right of the purple bottle, but not immediately to the right.

2. The red bottle is not next to the purple bottle.

3. The green bottle and the orange bottle are next to each other.

4. The orange bottle is next to the red bottle.

5. The poison is found in the bottle that is the second from the left.

Answers on page 241.

FIND THE WITNESS

On Washington Street, there are 5 houses. You need to follow up with a witness, Jennifer Brown, but without any address on the doors you are not sure which house to approach. You know that from a previous statement that Brown lives with her husband and stepdaughter. The staff at the corner coffee shop and your own observations give you some clues. From the information given, can you find the right house?

a. The Browns recently repainted their house white, like two other homes on their street.

b. There are two houses with kids living in them, and they are not adjacent.

c. House D is green and house C is blue.

d. House A has two kids living in it.

House A   House B   House C   House D   House E

Answer on page 241.

REMEMBERING THE SCENE
PART I

You will be grilled on the witness stand for your testimony in the case, and you'll want to answer each question accurately. Read over your case notes, then turn the page and see how much you remember.

The burglary and assault took place on Monday morning, March 14. The homeowner, Daniel J. Farsnooth, had been knocked out by burglars when he returned home after his morning run, interrupting the in-progress burglary. They subsequently fled the scene of the crime.

Farsnooth lives alone. He has owned the house for three years. He runs regularly at the same time every morning (leaving his house approximately 6:30 AM, returning 7:15 AM, before leaving again for work at 8 AM).

There was blood (Farsnooth's) in the foyer in three different locations. An umbrella stand had been knocked over in the struggle. Three hairs were found that might belong to the robbers.

One partial muddy shoeprint had been left on the entryway rug; it did not match any of the shoes in Farsnooth's closet, but he had had friends over on Sunday for a barbecue and said it could have been left on Sunday.

According to Farsnooth, all missing items in the house had been taken from the living room. He listed the following items as stolen: one DVD player; 3 DVDs (*The Martian; Star Wars: The Force Awakens; Captain America: Civil War*); stack of mail, including a credit card application and multiple ads; decorative clock, approximate value $75-100; one laptop. The TV had been moved to the edge of its stand.

According to Farsnooth, the front door was closed but probably not locked when he returned to the house after running. He went to unlock it automatically, but he noted that the door did not open when he did so, and he had to try again. This led him to believe later that it had been unlocked and was the point of entry for the thieves. There were no other signs of forced entry at any of the doors.

He had not seen anything out of place when he approached the house. There was no car parked in his driveway. There were multiple cars parked in the street, but he noted none that seemed out of place. He did not remember specifics about any of the cars on the street.

When he entered the house, he heard voices and saw two people wearing black ski masks, dressed in black, rushing at him. After a scuffle, one of them hit him on the head, and he fell down. The robbers ran past him through the open front door and fled on foot. He heard a car start up shortly afterward. He identified their voices as male, no accent. They were both of medium height and slim build.

REMEMBERING THE SCENE PART II

(Do not read this until you have read the previous page!)

1. How many DVDS were stolen?

   A. 1

   B. 2

   C. 3

   D. 4

2. The TV was stolen as well.

   ____ True

   ____ False

3. A partial fingerprint was found in the foyer.

   ____ True

   ____ False

4. Farsnooth's wife was away on vacation when the robbers came.

   ____ True

   ____ False

5. How many robbers were there?

   A. 1

   B. 2

   C. 3

   D. Unknown

6. A clock was stolen. What was its approximate value?

   A. $10

   B. $50

   C. $75

   D. $500

Answers on page 241.

SEEN AT THE SCENE
PART I

Study this picture of the crime scene for 1 minute, then turn the page.

SEEN AT THE SCENE
PART II

(Do not read this until you have read the previous page!)
Which image exactly matches the picture from the previous page?

1.

2.

3.

4.

Answer on page 241.

THE GEM THIEF

A company that sold gems found that 5 types of gems had been stolen from their warehouse. There was 1 gem of the first type, 2 of the second type, 3 of the third type, 4 of the fourth type, and 5 of the fifth type. From the information given below, can you tell how many gemstones of each kind were taken?

1. Either pearls or amethysts are the most plentiful gem.

2. There are fewer than three pieces of turquoise.

3. There are two more sapphires than pieces of jade.

4. There is one more amethyst than pieces of jade.

Answers on page 241.

TRACK THE FUGITIVE

The investigator is tracking the fugitive's past trips in order to find and recover information that was left behind in five cities. Each city was visited only once. Can you put together the travel timeline, using the information below?

1. Panama City was neither the first nor the final city on the list.

2. Caracas was either the first or third city.

3. Quito was visited sometime after La Paz.

4. Montevideo is one of the final two cities.

5. From Venezuela, the fugitive went immediately to Ecuador's capital city.

Answers on page 242.

INTERCEPTION

You've intercepted a message between a criminal who fled and his accomplice. From other information, you know this is supposed to contain the location of a key to a safe deposit box. But the message doesn't seem to make sense! Can you discover where the key is found?

IRON SARI DECIDE

OVER AGAIN GLUE

VIA SIDE

Answer on page 242.

JUST ONE MORE HEIST

Use the clues to change just one letter on each line to go from the top word to the bottom word. Do not change the order of the letters. You must have a common English word at each step.

DANNY

_____ peachy

_____ readily available

_____ applause

_____ music maker (plural)

_____ gives in

_____ used for some jewelry

_____ some nails

_____ alum (plural)

_____ pushes

_____ they get blamed

_____ they can keep you warm

_____ carries on a conversation

_____ tobacco units

_____ breaking down food

_____ the mating game?

_____ cardshark, for one

_____ it grips the ground

_____ may be cedar

_____ like G-rated jokes

_____ a New York city

OCEAN

Answers on page 242.

OVERHEARD INFORMATION
PART I

Read the story below, then turn the page and answer the questions.

The detective overheard the jewelry thief tell her accomplice about the different places where she stashed the loot. She said, "The gold bars are in a sack in the treehouse at the farm. The diamonds are taped to a closed vent in the front room of the Chicago two-flat. The ruby choker is in a sack of flour in the pantry at the condo. The emeralds are in the safety deposit box at the bank on Fourth Street."

OVERHEARD INFORMATION
PART II

(Do not read this until you have read the previous page!)
The investigator overheard the information about where
the stolen loot was stored, but didn't have anywhere
to write it down! Answer the questions below to help the
investigator remember.

1. **What is found in a treehouse?**

    A. Gold bars

    B. Diamonds

    C. Rubies

    D. Emeralds

2. **What is found in a sack of flour?**

    A. Ruby bracelet

    B. Ruby choker

    C. Ruby ring

    D. Emeralds

3. **The diamonds are found in this building.**

    A. Farmhouse

    B. Two-flat

    C. Condo

    D. Bank

4. **The bank is found here.**

    A. Fourth Street

    B. Fourth Avenue

    C. Fourth Drive

    D. We are not told.

Answers on page 242.

CRIME QUIZ

What does each abbreviation or acronym stand for?

1. DB

_____

2. LKA

_____

3. GSW

_____

4. DOC

_____

5. ATL

_____

Answers on page 242.

THE CAR THIEF

Litchfield County Police are investigating five classic car thefts which took place over the last two weeks. Each car was a different model and year, and no two cars were stolen from the same town. Using only the clues below, determine each stolen car's production year, model and owner, and determine the town in which each theft took place.

1. The Mustang, the 1978 model and the car stolen from Deerfield had three different owners.

2. The 1972 model year car wasn't stolen from Montclair, Deerfield or Kearney.

3. Of the Mustang and the car stolen from Montclair, one was a 1975 model and the other belonged to Dennis.

4. Thomas has never owned a Camaro.

5. Of Thomas's car and the one stolen from Taunton, one was the 1966 model and the other was the Mustang.

6. Jennifer's car wasn't stolen from Taunton or Deerfield.

7. The car stolen from Deerfield is three years newer than the one stolen from Ridgewood.

8. The Corvette was stolen from Main Street in Kearney.

9. Beatrice's car wasn't a 1969 model, and it wasn't stolen from Montclair.

10. The 1969 model year car is neither the Camaro nor the Continental.

		Models					Owners					Towns				
		Camaro	Continental	Corvette	Mustang	Thunderbird	Beatrice	Dennis	Irving	Jennifer	Thomas	Deerfield	Kearney	Montclair	Ridgewood	Taunton
Years	1966															
	1969															
	1972															
	1975															
	1978															
Towns	Deerfield															
	Kearney															
	Montclair															
	Ridgewood															
	Taunton															
Owners	Beatrice															
	Dennis															
	Irving															
	Jennifer															
	Thomas															

Years	Models	Owners	Towns
1966			
1969			
1972			
1975			
1978			

Answers on page 242.

WOMEN IN BLUE

ACROSS

1. Friday or Bilko: abbr.
4. Kind of talk or rally
7. Otherwise
12. Atlantic City casino, with "The"
13. Clean air org.: abbr.
14. Tree stand
15. Mark the beginning of
17. Lint locale
18. Cop show with Angie Dickinson
20. Squashes a squeak
21. Historic realm of Europe: abbr.
22. Little shavers
24. Twists the arm of
28. Last of a drink
29. Federal oversight group: abbr.
30. Need to pay the piper
31. Haifa inhabitant
34. Knock-down-drag-out
36. JFK's predecessor: inits.
37. Like a Burns acquaintance
38. Cop show with Holly Hunter
42. Thigh-length skirts
43. Send through the skies
45. "_____ it goes"
46. Shine, in some ads
47. Sign of a hit: abbr.
48. City in the Ruhr valley
49. Baste, in a way
50. Brain test: abbr.

DOWN

1. "Fifth Beatle" Sutcliffe
2. Suck air
3. Cop show with Heather Locklear
4. Pauline's problems
5. Iliad and Odyssey
6. Window piece
7. Turn a deaf ear
8. Constitution writer
9. Temporary superstar
10. Roasting place
11. _____ Aviv
16. Peace Nobelist Wiesel

19. "Wait just a minute!"

22. Mai _____

23. NFL gains: abbr.

24. Cop show with Marg Helgenberger

25. Cop show with Kathryn Morris

26. Ram's partner

27. "Got it?"

29. Narrow valley

32. Counsel

33. He made light work

34. Journalist Edward R.

35. Jack of old oaters

37. Fleet-footed

38. Major no-nos

39. Interjects

40. Comics' bits

41. Emerald isle

42. Investors' Fannie

44. Kirk's journal

Answers on page 243.

HISTORICAL MURDERERS

Every word listed is contained within the group of letters. Words can be found in a straight line horizontally, vertically, or diagonally. They may be read either forward or backward.

ANULA (This ancient queen regnant poisoned four husbands around 50 BC.)

CATHERINE MONVOISIN (Monvoison was burned at the stake in 1620, accused of poisonings and the ritual murder of more than 1,000 people.)

CHRISTMAN GENIPPERTEINGA (This German bandit from the 1500s reportedly killed more than 950 people, and was trying for 1,000.)

ELIZABETH BATHORY (This Hungarian noblewoman tortured and killed hundreds of girls, earning herself the name "The Blood Countess.")

GILLES DE RAIS (This French nobleman who lived ~1405–1440 is believed to have claimed more than 140 child victims.)

JASPER HANEBUTH (This highwayman from the 1600s was active in Eilinriede Forest.)

LEWIS HUTCHINSON (This Scot from the 1700s was known as "The Mad Doctor of Edinburgh Castle.")

LOCUSTA OF GAUL (She made poisons for Nero around 55 AD, but was executed by his successor.)

PETER STUMMP (Called "The Werewolf of Bedburg," he was accused of cannibalism and witchcraft.)

THUG BEHRAM (This leader of the Thuggee group of robbers and murderers lived in India in the early 1800s.)

```
A R P Z E L I Z A B E T H B A T H O R Y H W E
G W Q J O B W N H Z B L I H E M S C U H H A E
N O L I Q A N J P M B Z S Q G A T X Y L X S N
I U W X N L U A Q M P O H V L U O S L U K N I
E U T Y E Q K S W A E W Y U J K I U Q A N L S
T E I S H J W P G J J G N Y O K N G Q G A G I
R L W R Q X L E I U S A R K B K O P O F I C O
E A J P T A T R L Y Q U K U T I S F H O Q H V
P P N H A T R H L E A K T A C K N V C A K V N
P O X U K I G A E F Y X P T F D I P Z T O U O
I T E A Z M G N S E Q C M C D T H C R S P D M
N B B Q F Y Z E D V N C M L R C C O C U H J E
E G P K K U A B E W F L U I U V T T N C W E N
G W U C T D S U R D C K T U M Q U L F O F K I
N Q D B G L G T A P D J S A Y I H I P L W A R
A G H Z C I W H I J I G R M P L S C F F G Q E
M L V M J V P E S K E H E M L B I R B C U G H
T S H F P A W L P E E A T G C Q W Q R A A Z T
S C I L C O R T Z B M L E K G G E H O Y D C A
I O J P E N X K G Q C M P C C O L E O B O R C
R T Y E X G X U P O N C K A G U K B V Z P H A
H X V I I V H S W I H P K R W Y E D W U R D V
C H V I I T C C S R I G S V K K U W Y H U M I
```

Answers on page 243.

MOTEL HIDEOUT

A thief hides out in one of the 45 motel rooms listed in the chart below. The motel's in-house detective received a sheet of four clues, signed "The Logical Thief." Using these clues, the detective found the room number within 15 minutes—but by that time, the thief had fled. Can you find the thief's motel room more quickly?

1. Neither digit is 3.

2. The sum of the digits is either 5, 7, or 10.

3. If the digits were flipped, the resulting number would be found on the chart.

4. The number is prime.

51	52	53	54	55	56	57	58	59
41	42	43	44	45	46	47	48	49
31	32	33	34	35	36	37	38	39
21	22	23	24	25	26	27	28	29
11	12	13	14	15	16	17	18	19

Answer on page 243.

SEEN AT THE SCENE PART I

Study this picture of the crime scene for 1 minute, then turn the page.

SEEN AT THE SCENE
PART II

(Do not read this until you have read the previous page!)
Which image exactly matches the picture from the previous page?

1.   2.

3.   4.

Answer on page 243.

CRIME ANAGRAMS

Unscramble each word or phrase below to reveal a word or phrase related to criminal charges.

GRAY BLUR

TAUNT GODFATHER

SCARCE SOY

BY BRIER

HURL MAGENTAS

SPICY ACORN

RECREATE KING

SESSION OP

Answers on page 243.

TRACK THE FUGITIVE

The investigator is tracking the fugitive's past trips in order to find and recover information that was left behind in five cities. Each city was visited only once. Can you put together the travel timeline, using the information below?

1. From San Diego the fugitive went directly to the other city in California.

2. The fugitive went from Butte, Montana, to Des Moines, Iowa, but not directly. There was a stop in between.

3. Cleveland, Ohio, was one of the first two cities visited.

4. Sacramento was one of the final two cities visited.

5. When the fugitive arrived in Cleveland, it was from the West.

Answers on page 243.

IT'S IN THE BLOOD
PART I

Read the following information about the eight major blood types, then turn the page for a quiz.

1. O+: 38 percent: Can be given to a person with A+, B+, AB+, or O+ blood. A person with O+ blood can receive blood from O+ or O- donors.

2. A+: 34 percent: A person with A+ blood can receive A+, A-, O+, or O- blood. However, A+ blood can be given only to a person with the A+ or AB+ blood types.

3. B+: 9 percent: Can be given only to those with AB+ or B+ blood. Can receive blood from B+, B-, O+, or O- donors.

4. O-: 7 percent: The universal donor can be given to anyone. However, a person with the O- blood type can receive blood only from other O- donors.

5. A-: 6 percent: Can be given to a person with AB-, A-, AB+, or A+. Can only receive blood from O- or A- donors.

6. AB+: 3 percent: People with this blood type can receive blood of any type. But AB+ blood can only be given to a person who also has AB+ blood.

7. B-: 2 percent: B- blood can be given to those with B-, AB-, B+, or AB+ blood. A person with B- blood can receive blood from O- or B- blood types.

8. AB-: 1 percent: A person with this type can give blood to AB+ or AB- blood types, but must receive blood from O-, A-, B-, and AB- blood types.

IT'S IN THE BLOOD
PART II

(Do not read this until you have read the previous page!)

1. Which blood type is more common?

    _____ A+

    _____ A-

2. Is O positive or O negative the universal donor?

    _____ O+

    _____ O-

3. People with this blood type are considered the universal recipient.

    _____ A-

    _____ AB+

    _____ AB-

    _____ O+

4. This is the least common blood type.

    _____ A-

    _____ AB+

    _____ AB-

    _____ O+

5. People with O + blood can receive blood from O- donors.

    _____ True

    _____ False

Answers on page 244.

MURDER IN COLORADO

Cryptograms are messages in substitution code. Break the code to read the message. For example, THE SMART CAT might become FVO QWGDF JGF if F is substituted for T, V for H, O for E, and so on.

OAS LSHRSM NOMQHXFSM EBFFSL PJ
OI CBRS TIGSH ZSOTSSH 1894 QHL 1903.
OAS EBFFSM GQV AQRS GPMLSMSL Q
WFQBMRIVQHO TAI AQL NPJJINSLFV XBRSH
BHCIMGQOBIH OI OAS QPOAIMBOBSN; NAS
TQN CIPHL LSQL, NOMQHXFSL. QFOAIPXA
NSRSMQF GSH TSMS NPNJSWON, OAS
LSHRSM NOMQHXFSM TQN HSRSM
BLSHOBCBSL.

Answer on page 244.

DNA SEQUENCE

Examine the two images below carefully. Are these sequences a match or not?

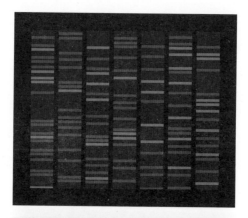

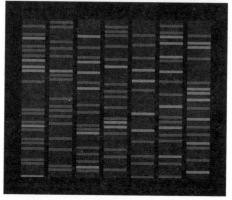

Answer on page 244.

THE SUSPECT FLED TO...

The letters in LONDON can be found in boxes 3, 10, 16, and 26, but not necessarily in that order. The same is true for the other cities listed below. Insert all the letters of the alphabet into the boxes. If you do this correctly, the shaded cells will reveal another world city.

Hint: Look for words that share a single letter. For example, ROME shares an O with SOFIA and an E with QUEBEC.

BRUSSELS: 7, 9, 18, 19, 21, 26

COPENHAGEN: 1, 3, 4, 5, 6, 16, 18, 24

HELSINKI: 1, 8, 9, 13, 16, 18, 26

JAKARTA: 2, 6, 7, 13, 20

LONDON: 3, 10, 16, 26

MEXICO CITY: 3, 4, 8, 15, 18, 20, 22, 23

QUEBEC: 4, 14, 18, 19, 21

QUEZON CITY: 3, 4, 8, 14, 15, 16, 17, 18, 19, 20

REYKJAVIK: 2, 6, 7, 8, 11, 13, 15, 18

ROME: 3, 7, 18, 23

SANTIAGO: 3, 6, 8, 9, 16, 20, 24

SOFIA: 3, 6, 8, 9, 12

VILNIUS: 8, 9, 11, 16, 19, 26

WARSAW: 6, 7, 9, 25

1	2	3	4	5	6	7	8	9	10	11	12	13

14	15	16	17	18	19	20	21	22	23	24	25	26

Answers on page 244.

INTERCEPTION

You've intercepted a message between a criminal who fled and his accomplice. It might be the criminal's current location, but there are four place names listed. Can you discover the criminal's current location hidden in the message?

ALGIERS

SEOUL

FORT WORTH

IDAHO

Answer on page 244.

WHAT CHANGED?
PART I

Study this picture of the crime scene for 1 minute, then turn the page.

WHAT CHANGED?
PART II

(Do not read this until you have read the previous page!)
From memory, can you tell what changed between this page and the previous page?

Answer on page 245.

DETECTIVE WORK!

Oh no! The museum has been raided and left a real mess! The detective has created a list of the museum's most valuable items. Can you find as many of these items as possible and discover which ones have been stolen?

Answers on page 245.

A CRIMINALLY GOOD QUOTE

To complete the word search, you will have to determine
the missing letters in the center of the grid. Once you have
revealed those letters, you will discover a quotation from
professional criminal Willie Sutton.

AARON BURR

ARCTURUS

BURGLAR

BUTCHER BLOCK

CHEAP SEATS

COAT OF ARMS

DO-IT-YOURSELFER

EARLYISH

EYEBROWS

FITZGERALD

FREEDOM FIGHTERS

GASHOUSE GANG

GO IT ALONE

HARD TO IMAGINE

IN WRITING

KING CRAB

KNEEPADS

LEGAL ASSISTANT

LEMON DROP

MALCOLM

NED BEATTY

OFF COURSE

ON BEHALF OF

ORANGEADE

SEES RED

SKI RESORT

SNOWSHOES

SOCIOLOGICALLY

SOFTBALL FIELD

THE IN CROWD

TOM BROKAW

TUMMYACHE

UNAWARE

U.S. HISTORY

VICIOUSNESS

WEB BROWSER

```
T O B L U R D L A R E G Z T I F M H
N R F C H E A P S E A T S T T A S C
A A O F R E F L E S R U O Y T I O D
T N V S C A P U H W S M H L Y I D E
S G E F E O T O Y O B M A L C O L M
I E J D A R U L N R R Y R A K U E V
S A B E B S           R C G N I K
S D A P E E           L I I C F C
A E N G Y G           I G I Z L O
L R A N D W           A O R E L L
A N C I E U           U L M U A B
G O I T A L           C O F F B R
E X O I U H N R B O N S N I P O T E
L E M R S R B I T E C D T C U S F H
E R A W A N U D S M R A F O T A O C
C Y O N O F R S P O O L I S R H S T
U N V I G A R L P S W O R B E Y E U
S R E T H G I F M O D E E R F A X B
```

Answers on page 245.

TRACK THE FUGITIVE

The investigator is tracking the fugitive's past trips in order to find and recover information that was left behind in five cities. Each city was visited only once. Can you put together the travel timeline, using the information below?

1. Skopje was visited sometime before Stockholm.

2. Riyadh was visited sometime after Seoul, but not immediately after.

3. Dodoma was one of the first three cities visited.

4. None of the cities that start with S were visited back to back.

Answers on page 245.

MOTEL HIDEOUT

A thief hides out in one of the 45 motel rooms listed in the chart below. The motel's in-house detective received a sheet of four clues, signed "The Logical Thief." Using these clues, the detective found the room number within 15 minutes—but by that time, the thief had fled. Can you find the thief's motel room more quickly?

1. The sum of the digits is 2, 4, 6, or 8.

2. One of the digits is larger than 4.

3. The number is prime.

4. If you flip the digits, the resulting number will be greater than 50.

51	52	53	54	55	56	57	58	59
41	42	43	44	45	46	47	48	49
31	32	33	34	35	36	37	38	39
21	22	23	24	25	26	27	28	29
11	12	13	14	15	16	17	18	19

Answer on page 245.

EITHER/OR

Complete the sentence with two words that are anagrams of each other (e.g. CARE and RACE).

If an inmate _____ too far, the _____ are there to corral him.

Answers on page 246.

SHOPLIFTING

Change just one letter on each line to go from the top word to the bottom word. Do not change the order of the letters. You must have a common English word at each step.

SHOP

_____

_____

_____

_____

LIFT

Answers on page 246.

SEEN AT THE SCENE
PART I

Study this picture of the crime scene for 1 minute, then turn the page.

SEEN AT THE SCENE
PART II

(Do not read this until you have read the previous page!)
Which image exactly matches the picture from the previous page?

1.

2.

3.

4.

Answer on page 246.

CRIME QUIZ

What does each abbreviation or acronym stand for?

1. B & E

_____

2. ADW

_____

3. DWI

_____

4. FTA

_____

5. GTA

_____

Answers on page 246.

THE EMBEZZLER

Courtney Crunk, a high-powered executive who has worked at a number of different Fortune 500 companies over the last decade, is suspected to have embezzled large sums of money from five of her most recent employers. Help the federal prosecutor build a case against Courtney by determining how much money she stole, and match each of those companies to its location and industry.

1. The five companies are: Centrafour, the one that reported $2 million in embezzled funds, and the three companies in telephony, logistics and web hosting.

2. Of Dynacorp and the company based out of New York, one is focused on logistics and the other reported $2 million in embezzled funds.

3. The mobile app company lost more money than Melcisco.

4. The company based out of Portland is either the one that lost $1 million or Dynacorp.

5. Courtney Crunk stole either $1 million or $8 million from the microchip manufacturer over a period of nine months.

6. Centrafour isn't headquarterEd in Chicago.

7. The company based in Atlanta lost half as much money as Wexica Incorporated.

8. Of Melcisco and the company based in Portland, one is focused on web hosting and the other reported $4 million stolen in 2020.

9. Courtney didn't steal exactly $1 million from the Atlanta company.

		Companies					Locations					Industries				
		Centrafour	Dynacorp	Melcisco	Truetel	Wexica Inc.	Atlanta	Boston	Chicago	New York	Portland	logistics	microchips	mobile apps	telephony	web hosting
Amounts	$500,000															
	$1,000,000															
	$2,000,000															
	$4,000,000															
	$8,000,000															
Industries	logistics															
	microchips															
	mobile apps															
	telephony															
	web hosting															
Locations	Atlanta															
	Boston															
	Chicago															
	New York															
	Portland															

Amounts	Companies	Locations	Industries
$500,000			
$1,000,000			
$2,000,000			
$4,000,000			
$8,000,000			

Answers on page 246.

THE BURKE AND HARE MURDERS

In the 1800s, William Burke and William Hare were two men supplying cadavers for anatomical study to Dr. Robert Knox. They eventually began killing people in order to receive extra payment. Every word listed is contained within the group of letters. Words can be found in a straight line horizontally, vertically, or diagonally. They may be read either forward or backward.

ANATOMY

CADAVERS

CORPSES

DISSECTION

EDINBURGH

GRAVE ROBBING

LODGERS

MARGARET DOCHERTY
(final victim)

MEDICAL RESEARCH

MURDER

RESURRECTION MEN

ROBERT KNOX

SCOTLAND

SIXTEEN VICTIMS

SUFFOCATION

WILLIAM BURKE

WILLIAM HARE

```
S U F F O C A T I O N S R O Y S N S D
W I L L I A M B U R K E S G R A O Y Z
E T J V I W M E D I N B U R G H I Y X
F S C A K W E G X Q K O M U U T T R B
R M I B G X D N N N S O N S Z R C N J
E I I D Y X I D I I F R L T E P E E Q
R T L J N F C G C Z B M E H G O S M S
A C O O C T A I M X U B C G J P S N R
H I O N J A L P P C Q O O J D F I O E
M V N R I C R M U R D E R R G O D I V
A N R X P H E D O T U Q L C E E L T A
I E N F D S S B E D K N Y J D V J C D
L E H R F E E R Y Y A A X N C D A E A
L T A L N R A S D R C Z A U F Y C R C
I X X Q T G R H Z L K L J G T T X R G
W I X K R O C R W E T U V H Z K Q U N
Q S N A S O H K W O W X W X P K W S I
L O M Y Q I V J C Y M O T A N A U E U
X X C N Y W K S X X M Y A R O X P R M
```

Answers on page 246.

MURDER IN UTAH

Cryptograms are messages in substitution code. Break the code to read the message. For example, THE SMART CAT might become FVO QWGDF JGF if F is substituted for T, V for H, O for E, and so on.

KOPJBCQ AZOIPJJ UPQ P MPQRLO—PJV

P ISOVZOZO. HLOJ BCOBP 1850, AZ ILTZV

RL RAZ SJCRZV QRPRZQ KOLI ZJGFPJV.

ACQ KCOQR RUL UCTZQ VCZV SJVZO

QSQMCBCLSQ BCOBSIQRPJBZQ. AZOIPJJ

FPRZO ISOVZOZV RUL ULIZJ CJ QPFR FPEZ

BCRX. JLR FLJG PKRZO RAZCO VZPRAQ,

AZ KFZV QPFR FPEZ BCRX PJV ZQBPMZV

DSQRCBZ, ZTPVCJG BPMRSOZ.

Answer on page 247.

DNA SEQUENCE

Examine the two images below carefully. Are these sequences a match or not?

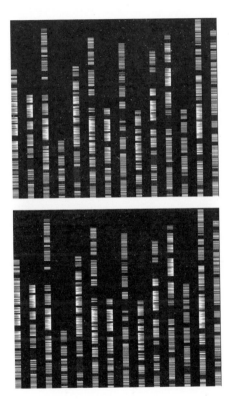

Answer on page 247.

FINGERPRINT MATCH

Find the matching fingerprint(s). There may be more than one.

Answer(s) on page 247.

PICK YOUR POISON

There are five bottles before you, but they've gotten jumbled up. Poison is found in one of them. If you arrange them from left to right, following the instructions given below, you will be able to know where the poison is found.

1. The poison is not found in the far left bottle or the bottle next to the far right bottle.

2. The red bottle is not next to the middle bottle.

3. The orange bottle is two bottles away from the bottle with the poison.

4. The green bottle is to the immediate left of the yellow bottle.

5. The blue bottle is immediately to the right of the red bottle.

6. The orange bottle is not found on either end.

Answers on page 247.

INTERCEPTION

You've intercepted a message between a criminal who fled and his accomplice. But the message doesn't seem to make sense! Can you discover the criminal's current location hidden in the message?

TAKE RIGHT AT INN, NO?

DRIVE EAST PARTWAY ON TRAIN

FLY IN VERY EXCITED

AND MOVE.

Answer on page 247.

FIND THE WITNESS

On Plum Street, there are 5 houses. You need to follow up with a witness, Melanie Shah, but the paperwork only lists her street, not the specific address. You know that Shah is a divorced woman who lives by herself. The staff at the coffee shop around the corner and your own observations give you some clues. From the information given, can you find the right house?

a. One member of the wait staff says Shah recently mentioned repainting her house blue. There are two blue houses on the street.

b. Another member of the wait staff knows that a family lives in house D.

c. House B is yellow.

d. House C is green.

e. House E is white.

House A   House B   House C   House D   House E

Answer on page 247.

A CASE OF ARSON
PART I

Read the account of the crime, then turn the page to answer questions.

On Saturday December 9th at 3:17 AM, a passing trucker reported a blaze at a structure on Faraday Road. Firefighters found a fire at the empty office building at 514 E. Faraday Road. The office were rented by an app developer, and consisted of five rooms: an entry room, three offices, a bathroom, and one storage closet. The blaze was set in the storage closet.

Four employees worked out of this office: Tomas Villanueva, lead developer; Rembert Whitehead, audio developer; Rachel Smith, junior developer; Yvette Washington, marketing. Another junior developer had been recently fired for cause: Thomas Greene.

No chemicals or flammable materials were kept in the storage closet. Investigation revealed that turpentine was used as an accelerant; all employees agreed that none was found anywhere in the office.

There were no signs of forced entry. The external door to the building and the main door to each set of offices were opened by electronic keycard. Current keycards were in the possession of current employees, the building owner, and the cleaning crew.

Attention focused on current and ex-employees of the app developers. All professed to be happy with their employment. Washington brought up an ex-boyfriend (Tim Tresworth, one charge of drunk and disorderly at age 21, one dropped charge of shoplifting at the age of 22, no record of arson) who had gotten "borderline stalkery" when they broke up 6 months ago. He no longer had access to her keycard, but he would have had access to her purse while they were dating, and might have duplicated it then.

When interviewed, Tresworth expressed anger at Washington for "trying to get him involved" He said he had moved on and was dating someone new. He professed to have been at her house the night of the fire. His current girlfriend, Janet Parkinson, confirmed.

Thomas Greene, former employee, no prior convictions, was let go for not meeting deadlines, not responding well to feedback, and not working well with outside clients. Greene said that he had not been given clear directions or support and that he'd been set up to fail, and that by the time he was fired he was glad to leave the company. He had since been doing freelance work. He had turned in his keycard to Villanueva (Villanueva confirmed).

A half-full container of turpentine was found in his apartment, in a closet in the guest bedroom, behind a stack of blank canvases. He attested that it was left behind from a girlfriend who had painted oils. There was no dust on the canister; no fingerprints were found.

A CASE OF ARSON
PART II

(Do not read this until you have read the previous page!)

1. The fire could have been accidental.
   - _____ Likely
   - _____ Unlikely

2. There were signs of forced entry.
   - _____ True
   - _____ Unfonfirmed
   - _____ False

3. Thomas Greene had a working keycard for the building.
   - _____ True
   - _____ Unfonfirmed
   - _____ False

4. Tresworth had an alibi for the time of the crime.
   - _____ True
   - _____ Unfonfirmed
   - _____ False

5. The turpentine found in Greene's apartment was left behind by an ex-girlfriend.
   - _____ True
   - _____ Unfonfirmed
   - _____ False

Answers on page 248.

MOTEL HIDEOUT

A thief hides out in one of the 45 motel rooms listed in the chart below. The motel's in-house detective received a sheet of four clues, signed "The Logical Thief." Using these clues, the detective found the room number within 15 minutes—but by that time, the thief had fled. Can you find the thief's motel room more quickly?

1. If you multiply the digits together, the result will be a number on this chart.

2. The sum of the digits is greater than 9.

3. If you subtract the first digit from the second, the result is 5.

4. The number is not divisible by 19.

51	52	53	54	55	56	57	58	59
41	42	43	44	45	46	47	48	49
31	32	33	34	35	36	37	38	39
21	22	23	24	25	26	27	28	29
11	12	13	14	15	16	17	18	19

Answer on page 248.

FORGING MONEY

Change just one letter on each line to go from the top word to the bottom word. Do not change the order of the letters. You must have an English word at each step.

FORGE

_____

_____

_____ things in a front position or golfer's warnings

_____

_____

_____

_____

MONEY

Answers on page 248.

SEEN AT THE SCENE
PART I

Study this picture of the crime scene for 1 minute, then turn the page.

SEEN AT THE SCENE
PART II

(Do not read this until you have read the previous page!)
Which image exactly matches the picture from the previous page?

1.

2.

3.

4.

Answer on page 248.

CRIME ANAGRAMS

Unscramble each word or phrase below to reveal a word or phrase related to the courtroom.

SOUR COPTER

YON TATER

TANNED FED

I TRULY JAR

TIS SEWN

FAIL FIBS

FAINT FLIP

JUG RAN DRY

Answers on page 248.

THE GEM THIEF

A company that sold gems found that 6 types of gems had been stolen from their warehouse. There was 1 gem of the first type, 2 of the second type, 3 of the third type, 4 of the fourth type, 5 of the fifth type, and 6 of the sixth type. From the information given below, can you tell how many gemstones of each kind were taken?

1. There are either 2 emeralds or 2 amethysts.

2. There are either 3 or 4 pieces of jade.

3. Opals are either the most or least plentiful gem.

4. There is exactly one more peridot than pieces of jade, and at least two more pieces of jade than topaz.

5. There are even numbers of peridots and amethysts.

Answers on page 248.

TRACK THE FUGITIVE

The investigator is tracking the fugitive's past trips in order to find and recover information that was left behind in five cities. Each city was visited only once. Can you put together the travel timeline, using the information below?

1. Brussels and Moscow were separated by exactly two other cities. Either Brussels or Moscow could have been the earlier visit.

2. Ankara was not the third place visited.

3. Tunis and Athens were visited back to back, but not necessarily in that order.

4. The visit to Athens preceded the trip to Ankara, but not immediately.

5. One of the cities that starts with A was followed immediately by a trip to the city that starts with B.

Answers on page 248.

MURDER METHODS

Every word listed is contained within the group of letters. Words can be found in a straight line horizontally, vertically, or diagonally. They may be read either forward or backward.

ARSON

ASPHYXIATE

BEAT

EXPLODE

GARROTE

GORE

GUILLOTINE

HIT

IMPALE

POISON

SHOOT

SKEWER

SMOTHER

STAB

STRANGLE

```
K A M O E T I H A X A N D E
C R I C T I M P A L E J R X
N S Q O O E D M H P A O F P
O O T Z R Z E L H A G R O E
O N A B R K N G S T W I D S
R M E H A J P P P M S O S N
F E B S G T H A P O L U S R
O X H I H Y S E N P V L T J
M E Y T X O J H X M Y Z R A
Y X J I O X O E T O P G A P
N P A Z L M J T U J Y A N M
W T V O B P S B Q J R Q G Z
E G G U I L L O T I N E L O
M Y G T Q P R E W E K S E W
```

Answers on page 249.

DNA SEQUENCE

Examine the two images below carefully. Are these sequences a match or not?

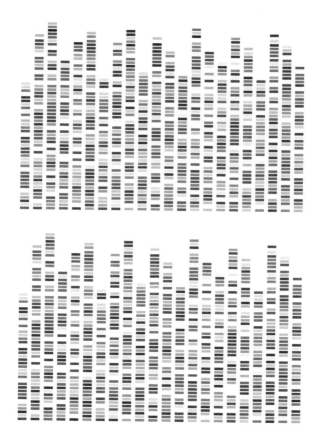

Answer on page 249.

WHAT DO YOU SEE?
PART I

Study this picture of the crime scene for 1 minute, then turn the page.

WHAT DO YOU SEE?
PART II

(Do not read this until you have read the previous page!)
Which image exactly matches the crime scene?

1

2

3

4

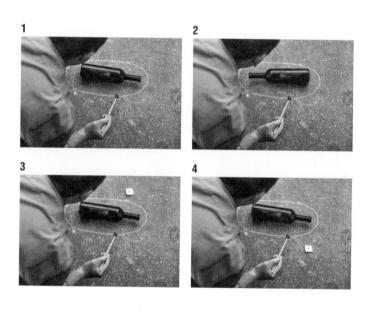

Answer on page 249.

INTERVIEWING WITNESSES

Use the following information to figure out who is lying and who is telling the truth. There are 2 truth tellers and 2 liars. You know that A is telling the truth.

Person A says person C is lying.

Person B says person D is lying.

Person C says person B is telling the truth.

Person D says person A is telling the truth.

Answers on page 249.

THE DOGNAPPER

Five purebred dogs have gone missing in just the last week, leading some to suspect that a single dognapper is to blame. Each of the five dogs went missing on a different day, and each was of a different breed. No two dogs belonged to the same family. Using only the clues below, match each of the five missing dogs to their breed and family, and determine the day on which each went missing.

1. The Jenkins family found their dog missing two days after the Voigts' dog was taken.

2. The bulldog went missing on either Monday or Friday.

3. The McHales' dog went missing sometime before the Albertsons' pooch.

4. The five dogs were Kenzie, the one that went missing on Thursday, the bulldog and the two owned by the Voigt and McHale families.

5. Of the Great Dane and the McHales' dog, one was Terry and the other went missing on Wednesday.

6. Benji disappeared two days after the Albertsons' dog (which wasn't the Chihuahua) was taken.

7. Sanjay Singh's dog was stolen on Thursday morning.

8. Fido wasn't stolen on Wednesday.

9. Kenzie disappeared one day after the Pomeranian was taken.

		Breeds					Dogs					Families				
		Bulldog	Chihuahua	Great Dane	Pomeranian	Rottweiler	Benji	Fido	Kenzie	Lucille	Terry	Albertson	Jenkins	McHale	Singh	Voigt
Days	Monday															
	Tuesday															
	Wednesday															
	Thursday															
	Friday															
Families	Albertson															
	Jenkins															
	McHale															
	Singh															
	Voigt															
Dogs	Benji															
	Fido															
	Kenzie															
	Lucille															
	Terry															

Days	Breeds	Dogs	Families
Monday			
Tuesday			
Wednesday			
Thursday			
Friday			

Answers on page 249.

NOT QUITE A WANTED POSTER

Cryptograms are messages in substitution code. Break the code to read the message. For example, THE SMART CAT might become FVO QWGDF JGF if F is substituted for T, V for H, O for E, and so on.

UZNLFH ULI GSV XLIIFKGRLM RM SRH

KLORGRXZO NZXSRMV, DROORZN "YLHH"

GDVVW UOVW GL HKZRM DSROV LM

SLFHV ZIIVHG. SV DZH XZFTSG YVXZFHV

HLNVLMV GSVIV IVXLTMRAVW SRN WFV GL

KLORGRXZO XZIGLLMH GSZG HPVDVIVW

SRH XLIIFKG "GZNNZMB SZOO" NZXSRMV.

Answer on page 250.

WHAT CHANGED?
PART I

Study this picture of the crime scene for 1 minute, then turn the page.

WHAT CHANGED?
PART II

(Do not read this until you have read the previous page!)
From memory, can you tell what changed between this page and the previous page?

Answer on page 250.

You've intercepted a message between a criminal who fled and his accomplice. But the message doesn't seem to make sense! Can you discover the criminal's current location hidden in the message?

DRAB YOU STANDS

ALAS, EAT BANANA AT ALIBI ONTO THEN

AS ANTI BEAUX

JUMP, MUM

Answer on page 250.

TRIAL OF THE CENTURY 1927 EDITION, PART I

Read this true crime account, then turn to the next page to test your knowledge.

On that March morning in 1927, nine-year-old Lorraine Snyder found her mother Ruth, her hands and feet bound, begging for help in the hall outside her bedroom. The girl rushed to her neighbors in the New York City suburb, and they called the police.

What the police found was more terrible still. Ruth Snyder's husband Albert lay dead in the bedroom—his skull smashed, wire strung around his neck, and a chloroform-soaked cloth shoved up his nose. His 32-year-old widow told the police that a large man had knocked her out, stolen her jewelry, and assaulted her husband.

But the police found her jewels under a mattress; they also discovered a bloody pillowcase and a bloody, five-pound sash weight in a closet. As if this evidence wasn't damning enough, police located a check Ruth had written to Henry Judd Gray in the amount of $200. Gray's name was found in her little black book—along with the names of 26 other men. Little Lorraine told the cops that "Uncle Judd" had been in the home the previous night. A tie clip with the initials HJG was found on the floor.

The marriage had been unhappy for some time. Ruth Brown met Albert Snyder—14 years her senior, and her boss—in 1915. She and Albert married and had Lorraine, but their union was flawed from the start. Albert was still enthralled with his former fiancée of ten years ago, who had died. Ruth haunted the jazz clubs of Roaring Twenties Manhattan, drinking and dancing 'til the wee hours of the morning without her retiring spouse, whom she had dubbed "the old crab."

In 1925, the unhappy wife went on a blind date and met Judd Gray, a low-key corset salesperson. Soon the duo was meeting for afternoon trysts. Eventually, Ruth arranged for her unsuspecting husband to sign a life insurance policy worth more than $70,000. At the murder scene, the police questioned Ruth about Gray. It wasn't long before she had spilled her guts, though she claimed it was Gray who'd actually strangled Albert. Meanwhile, 33-year-old Gray was found at a hotel in Syracuse, New York. Gray quickly confessed but claimed it was Ruth who'd strangled Albert.

A month after the arrest, a brief trial ensued. For three weeks, the courtroom was jammed with 1,500 spectators. Ruth was given the moniker "The Blonde Butcher." Ruth and Gray were pronounced guilty after a 100-minute deliberation by an all-male jury. The pair were executed on January 12, 1928, by the electric chair.

TRIAL OF THE CENTURY 1927 EDITION, PART II

(Do not read this until you have read the previous page!)

1. The first name of the victim was:

   A. Albert

   B. Alfred

   C. Alphonse

   D. Snyder

2. Judd Gray left this behind at the murder scene:

   A. A pair of cufflinks with his initials

   B. A tie clip with his initials

   C. A pair of shoes

   D. An engraved pen

3. Ruth was called by this nickname

   A. Black Widow

   B. The Ruthless Widow

   C. The Blonde Butcher

   D. The Murderess

4. Ruth's daughter was named:

   A. Lorraine

   B. Loretta

   C. Lorrie

   D. Lauren

Answers on page 250.

SEEN AT THE SCENE
PART I

Study this picture of the crime scene for 1 minute, then turn the page.

SEEN AT THE SCENE
PART II

(Do not read this until you have read the previous page!)

1. The placards marking the bullets show these numbers:

   A. 1, 2, 3

   B. 1, 2, 3, 4

   C. 1, 2, 3, 5

   D. 1, 2, 3, 4, 5

2. The police car's front lights were:

   A. On

   B. Off

3. The police car's siren lights were:

   A. On

   B. Off

4. A knife was found at the scene.

   A. Yes

   B. No

Answers on page 250.

MOTEL HIDEOUT

A thief hides out in one of the 45 motel rooms listed in the chart below. The motel's in-house detective received a sheet of four clues, signed "The Logical Thief." Using these clues, the detective found the room number within 15 minutes—but by that time, the thief had fled. Can you find the thief's motel room more quickly?

1. The number is not divisible by 5 or 6.

2. If you subtract the first digit from the second, the result is 3 or greater.

3. The number is divisible by 7.

4. If you reversed the digits, the result would be a number found on the chart.

51	52	53	54	55	56	57	58	59
41	42	43	44	45	46	47	48	49
31	32	33	34	35	36	37	38	39
21	22	23	24	25	26	27	28	29
11	12	13	14	15	16	17	18	19

Answer on page 250.

THE GEM THIEF

A company that sold gems found that 6 types of gems had been stolen from their warehouse. There was 1 gem of the first type, 2 of the second type, 3 of the third type, 4 of the fourth type, 5 of the fifth type, and 6 of the sixth type. From the information given below, can you tell how many gemstones of each kind were taken?

1. There are three times as many pearls as sapphires.

2. There are three fewer agates than rubies.

3. There are even numbers of diamonds and turquoises.

4. There are more diamonds than turquoises.

Answers on page 251.

TRACK THE FUGITIVE

The investigator is tracking the fugitive's past trips in order to find and recover information that was left behind in five cities. Each city was visited only once. Can you put together the travel timeline, using the information below?

1. The fugitive went from Stockholm directly to the capital of Liechtenstein.

2. Vienna and the other city that started with V were neither the first nor last cities.

3. Paris was either the first or fourth city.

4. The trip to Berlin was preceded immediately by a trip to Vaduz.

Answers on page 251.

POLICE LINEUPS

Every word listed is contained within the group of letters. Words can be found in a straight line horizontally, vertically, or diagonally. They may be read either forward or backward.

ANONYMITY

BIAS

CONFIDENCE RATING

CULPRIT

FACING

FILLERS

IDENTITY PARADE

LOADING

ONE-WAY MIRROR

PHOTO ARRAY

PROFILE

PUTATIVE ID

SHOW-UP

SUSPECT

VICTIM

WITNESS

```
T I R P L U C I M Y N O N A C P
C G T R O R R I M Y A W E N O R
I A E P S U S W B I A S P N N O
V R R I U S U S P E C T L G F F
S E D A R A P Y T I T N E D I I
R C R P L N U T E L L I F H D L
E N A P H O T O A R R A Y P E F
L E P R T N A B C U L P R S N G
L D Y I S Y T D H S F M T P C N
I I S M H M I W I A S P A U E I
F F I Y O I V D C N R E W T R C
B N P A W T E I A O G I N A A A
I O N W U Y I L F O T C A T T F
A C E E P U D I S N L D G I I M
F B D N T A L E E S H O W V N W
E I I O C E V M I T C I V E G H
```

Answers on page 251.

WHEN YOU DON'T WANT YOUR 15 MINUTES OF FAME

Cryptograms are messages in substitution code. Break the code to read the message. For example, THE SMART CAT might become FVO QWGDF JGF if F is substituted for T, V for H, O for E, and so on.

PDC ORZFCBP KQ PDC SCNW QENOP

CLEOKYC KQ PDC PCHCSEOEKJ ODKT

"UICNEBU'O IKOP TUJPCY" EJ 1988, YUSEY

FUICO NKZCNPO DEY EJ DEO ULUNPICJP

QKN QKRN YUWO UQPCN OCCEJA DEO BUOC

LNKQEHCY KJ PCHCSEOEKJ. UIKJA KPDCN

BNEICO, NKZCNPO TUO BKJSEBPCY KQ

UNICY NKZZCNW UJY IRNYCN.

Answer on page 251.

OVERHEARD INFORMATION PART I

Read the story below, then turn the page and answer the questions.

While on a train, a bystander overheard a criminal tell an accomplice where a set of upcoming thefts would take place. The criminal said, "We're hitting up a bunch of stores on February 8, or February 10th if it snows on the 8th. But if it's raining, we're still on. This is the order: first the bakery on Lymon Street, then go to Marsh Street for the art gallery. Then we ditch the loot at the safehouse on Second Street before going across town to First Electronics on Fourth Street before going to ground."

OVERHEARD INFORMATION PART II

(Do not read this until you have read the previous page!)
The bystander overheard the information about the crimes that were planned, but didn't have anywhere to write it down! Answer the questions below to help the bystander remember what to tell the police.

1. **The first location will be:**
   A. A bakery
   B. An art gallery
   C. A safehouse, to get supplies
   D. An electronics store

2. **The theft will take place on this day**
   A. February 8
   B. February 9
   C. February 10
   D. February 12

3. **If it rains, the theft will take place on this day.**
   A. February 8
   B. February 9
   C. February 10
   D. February 12

4. **The electronics store is found on this street.**
   A. Lyman
   B. Marsh
   C. First
   D. Fourth

Answers on page 251.

CRIME ANAGRAMS

Unscramble each word or phrase below to reveal a word or phrase related to law enforcement lingo.

SLAT USA

PREPARE TORT

MEDIA SERMON

AEROSPACE BULB

CONTAIN FIR

SNOT CIRCA

I MEANT

BOAR POINT

Answers on page 252.

CRIME QUIZ

What does each abbreviation or acronym stand for?

1. BOLO

_____

2. APB

_____

3. KA

_____

4. DA

_____

5. UNSUB

_____

Answers on page 252.

WHAT CHANGED?
PART 1

Study this picture for 1 minute, then turn the page.

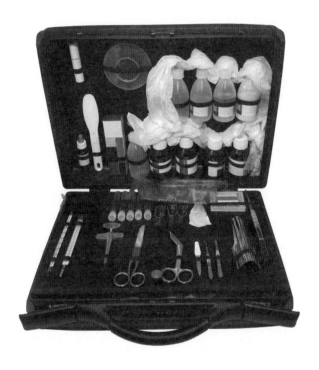

WHAT CHANGED? PART II

(Do not read this until you have read the previous page!)
From memory, can you tell what changed between this page and the previous page?

Answer on page 252.

LOOPY LAWS

Cryptograms are messages in substitution code. Break the code to read the message. For example, THE SMART CAT might become FVO QWGDF JGF if F is substituted for T, V for H, O for E, and so on.

FDDAOUJSI KA OJDG WQJKG JS "EAP DFS

ILK FOOLWKLU VAO KGFK," JK'W JXXLIFX

KA VFXX FWXLLR JS F DGLLWL VFDKAOE JS

WAPKG UFHAKF.

Answer on page 252.

ISABELLA'S MISSING COLLECTION

ACROSS

1. French forerunner of Impressionism
5. The perpendicular from the center of a regular polygon to one of the sides
11. Ardor
12. Zealous
13. In days gone by
14. It might be proper
15. El ___
16. Head, informally
17. Despite all the efforts, still not found
20. Gallery security worker
21. Legal exam
24. "Buenos ___!"
26. Percussion stick
27. PC monitor spec. of yore
30. Hitch on the run
32. Hawks support it
33. Drowsy
35. Opposite of gain
37. Frozen rain
39. Some finger foods
42. They hang as a theft reminders
46. Vb. form like "to be"
48. In place of
49. Wall-climbing equipment
50. Challenge, legally
51. Carrier to Israel
52. Mini-rage
53. Diatribes
54. Edgar who painted ballerinas

DOWN

1. List of food
2. Hop or sing ending
3. World's smallest republic
4. Nonet
5. Tel's follower
6. Yearned deeply
7. What fresheners fight
8. Wood shop tool
9. Object of some inflation

10. Crime organization members

12. Of some electrodes

18. Bawled

19. House wing

22. Film's Gardner

23. Netflix's "This Is a Robbery" topic

25. Costa del ___ (Spanish resort area)

26. Romero or Chavez

28. Supermodel Carangi

29. More concise

31. Amount of soup on the stove

34. Elegant tree

36. Like desert vegetation

38. Attendance counter

40. "Honor ___ thieves"

41. Brown shade used in old photos

43. Said 'guilty,' say

44. They're needed for passing

45. Complete collections

47. Rapa ___

Answers on page 252.

THE PONZI SCHEMERS

The SEC is currently investigating five Ponzi schemes masquerading as legitimate hedge funds. Each "fund" was begun in a different year and in a different city, and no two funds have the same total claimed assets. Using only the clues below, match each hedge fund to its headquarters (city), the year it was founded, and the total amount of assets each claims to have under its control.

1. The Alpha Sky fund was founded in either 2007 or 2019.

2. Of the Goldleaf fund and the one with over $200 million in claimed assets, one is headquartered in Seattle and the other was founded in 2019.

3. Both the Wellspring fund and the fund headquartered in Chicago (which are completely separate schemes) were founded sometime between 2005 and 2011.

4. The fund with $105 million in claimed assets was founded sometime after the one headquartered in Los Angeles, but not in 2016.

5. The Wellspring fund, the one based in Seattle, and the one started in 2016 are three different Ponzi schemes.

6. The Gemstone fund, which has more than $200 million in claimed assets, was started three years before the one based out of Miami.

7. The Concorde fund has more than $60 million in claimed assets.

8. The Ponzi scheme based out of Los Angeles doesn't claim to have exactly $50 million in assets.

	Assets					Headquarters					Hedge Funds				
	$32 million	$50 million	$79 million	$105 million	$225 million	Chicago	Dallas	Los Angeles	Miami	Seattle	Alpha Sky	Concorde	Gemstone	Goldleaf	Wellspring
Years 2007															
2010															
2013															
2016															
2019															
Hedge Funds Alpha Sky															
Concorde															
Gemstone															
Goldleaf															
Wellspring															
Headquarters Chicago															
Dallas															
Los Angeles															
Miami															
Seattle															

Years	Assets	Headquarters	Hedge Funds
2007			
2010			
2013			
2016			
2019			

Answers on page 252.

DNA SEQUENCE

Examine the two images below carefully. Are these sequences a match or not?

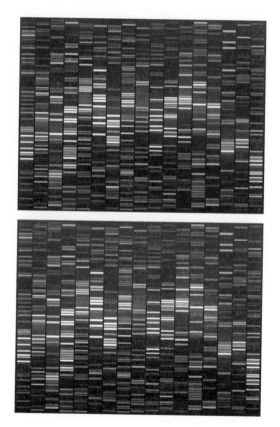

Answer on page 253.

PICK YOUR POISON

There are six bottles before you, but they've gotten jumbled up. Poison is found in one of them. If you arrange them from left to right, following the instructions given below, you will be able to know where the poison is found. From left to right, the spots where the bottles can be placed are numbered 1, 2, 3, 4, 5, 6.

1. There are two blue bottles. They are not next to each other, and neither contains the poison.

2. The poison is in an even-numbered bottle.

3. The purple bottle is to the right of the yellow bottle, with at least two other bottles separating them.

4. The poison is in either the yellow bottle or the red bottle.

5. Both blue bottles are to the left of the purple bottle, which is not on either end.

6. The orange bottle is to the left of the red bottle, but not necessarily the immediate left.

7. The poison is not in a bottle with a number that can be divided by 3.

8. The orange bottle is to the right of one of the blue bottles.

Answers on page 253.

INTERCEPTION

You've intercepted a message between a criminal who fled and his accomplice. But the message doesn't seem to make sense! Can you discover the criminal's current location hidden in the message?

BRO, SEE, EDIT, READ, DYE, REREAD.

OFF FLEW SIS, AGOG THAT OTHERS

STARTED FOR

ALL SAT.

Answer on page 253.

FIND THE WITNESS

You want to interview a witness in a cold case, Ken Rawlins. He and his wife have moved since the case was active. From their fomer neighbor, you know they now live on Perkins Avenue, which has five houses, but you don't know which house they live in. They do not have any children. The staff at the bakery around the corner and your own observations give you some clues. From the information given, can you find the right house?

1. There are married couples in two of the houses.

2. Kids live in the middle house and one of the houses next door.

3. An elderly widower lives in one of the corner houses.

4. A single mom with custody of her kids lives in house D.

5. A widow lives next door to the widower and they have recently begun dating.

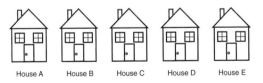

House A   House B   House C   House D   House E

Answer on page 253.

MAKING A LIST, CHECKING IT TWICE

Cryptograms are messages in substitution code. Break the code to read the message. For example, THE SMART CAT might become FVO QWGDF JGF if F is substituted for T, V for H, O for E, and so on.

TYEEYPF DYGLZV CONRCYGLHG TPL

NCZ ZQYNHK-YG-RCYZB BHK NCZ

YGNZKGPNYHGPE GZTL LZKSYRZ TCZG

CZ CPQ P RHGSZKLPNYHG TYNC A.

ZQMPK CHHSZK. NCZ BXY NZG FHLN

TPGNZQ BOMYNYSZ EYLN TPL XHKG BKHF

NCPN QYLROLLYHG. VZPKL ZPKEYZK,

CONRCYGLHG CPQ PELH XZZG P KZIHKNZK

PN NCZ BPFHOL LRHIZL NKYPE.

Answer on page 253.

FEMALE BANK ROBBERS PART I

Read this true crime account, then turn to the next page to test your knowledge.

The U.S. Department of Justice reports that fewer than 5 percent of all bank robbers are women and that women involved in bank robberies are more likely to be accomplices than ringleaders.

For a short two-year period, 1932–34, Bonnie Parker and Clyde Barrow captivated the nation by posing as that generation's Romeo and Juliet—on the lam. It is thought that Clyde and his "Barrow Gang" actually committed most of the crimes. Some in the gang claimed they never saw Bonnie fire a gun, even if she was frequently photographed brandishing weapons and self-parodying the gangster image. Their crime spree took them across several states, but the law finally caught up to them outside of Sailes, Louisiana, where the pair was killed in a gunfight.

Not quite as famous was Monica "Machine Gun Molly" Proietti from Quebec, Canada. A tiny woman of fewer than 100 pounds, Proietti was involved in more than 20 bank robberies during the 1960s, leading an all-male band of criminals. She was gunned down at age 27 after she and two accomplices robbed a bank and made off with $3,074.

FEMALE BANK ROBBERS
PART II

(Do not read this until you have read the previous page!)

1. About this percentage of bank robbers are women.

   A. 1%

   B. 5%

   C. 15%

   D. 45%

2. Bonnie's last name was:

   A. Parker

   B. Clyde

   C. Barrow

   D. Barker

3. Monica Proietti's nickname was:

   A. Big Nose

   B. Ma

   C. Machine Gun Monica

   D. Machine Gun Molly

4. Proietti was active in this decade.

   A. 1920s

   B. 1940s

   C. 1960s

   D. 1980s

Answers on page 253.

MOTEL HIDEOUT

A thief hides out in one of the 45 motel rooms listed in the chart below. The motel's in-house detective received a sheet of four clues, signed "The Logical Thief." Using these clues, the detective found the room number within 15 minutes—but by that time, the thief had fled. Can you find the thief's motel room more quickly?

1. Each digit is either a prime number or 1.

2. The number itself is not prime.

3. The second digit is larger than the first.

4. Add the digits together, and the result is divisible by both 3 and 4.

51	52	53	54	55	56	57	58	59
41	42	43	44	45	46	47	48	49
31	32	33	34	35	36	37	38	39
21	22	23	24	25	26	27	28	29
11	12	13	14	15	16	17	18	19

Answer on page 254.

THE GEM THIEF

A company that sold gems found that 6 types of gems had been stolen from their warehouse. There was 1 gem of the first type, 2 of the second type, 3 of the third type, 4 of the fourth type, 5 of the fifth type, and 6 of the sixth type. From the information given below, can you tell how many gemstones of each kind were taken?

1. There are either 3 or 6 pieces of jade.

2. There are either 2 or 5 pieces of topaz.

3. There is either 1 opal or there are 4 opals.

4. There are more emeralds than garnets, but garnets are not the least plentiful gem.

5. There are half as many aquamarines as pieces of jade.

6. There are not 5 emeralds.

Answers on page 254.

TRACK THE FUGITIVE

The investigator is tracking the fugitive's past trips in order to find and recover information that was left behind in five cities. Each city was visited only once. Can you put together the travel timeline, using the information below?

1. The fugitive did not travel from Austin to Dallas or vice versa.

2. The fugitive traveled to Portland from Nashville, with a stop at one other city in between.

3. The fugitive traveled from one city that starts with D immediately to the next, in alphabetical order.

4. Austin was not the last city visited.

5. Denver was one of the first three cities visited.

Answers on page 254.

THE GRAFFITI GANG

The town of Cordilla Hills has a serious graffiti problem. A gang of five graffiti artists has been spray painting their tags all over town. Law enforcement knows their individual names but they still need help to build a case against the gang. Help them out by matching each graffiti artist to his or her unique neighborhood, the two colors of paint they use (no two members use the same two colors) and the total number of graffiti tags each has painted.

1. Neither Daryl nor the graffiti artist who uses cyan and silver paint works Downtown.

2. Of Lucretia and the suspect who works on the East Side, one has 29 known tags and the other uses only orange and teal spray paint.

3. The person who uses cyan and silver paint (who isn't Clarence) has 14 more tags than whoever works Uptown, and 14 fewer tags than Agatha.

4. Lucretia has 7 fewer tags than the person who works exclusively with gray and purple spray paint.

5. The five suspects are Daryl, Lucretia, the person with 36 tags, the one who works in Midtown, and the one who uses cyan and silver paint.

6. The tags found in Midtown don't use green or white paint.

		Name					Neighborhood					Colors				
		Agatha	Clarence	Daryl	Lucretia	Patrick	Downtown	East Side	Midtown	Uptown	West Side	blue & pink	cyan & silver	gray & purple	green & white	orange & teal
Tags	15															
	22															
	29															
	36															
	43															
Colors	blue & pink															
	cyan & silver															
	gray & purple															
	green & white															
	orange & teal															
Neighborhood	Downtown															
	East Side															
	Midtown															
	Uptown															
	West Side															

Tags	Name	Neighborhood	Colors
15			
22			
29			
36			
43			

Answers on page 254.

STOLEN STREET SIGNS

Someone's been stealing street signs! Every week (always on a Saturday night) a new sign has gone missing. Each time it's a different type of sign (stop sign, yield sign, etc.) in a different part of town. Help the police track down the thief by matching each sign to the date it went missing and its original location at the intersection of two streets.

1. Of the speed limit sign and the one that was at Barnacle Road, one went missing on July 25th and the other was at the corner of Tarragon Lane.

2. Quinella Street doesn't intersect with Falstaff St.

3. The speed limit sign was stolen sometime after the one from Ralston Avenue.

4. The Amble Lane sign didn't go missing on August 1st.

5. The Dwight Street sign went missing one week before the one from Tarragon Lane.

6. The one-way sign was stolen 1 week before the Casper Boulevard sign, and 3 weeks before the one on Selby Street.

7. The dead end sign, the stop sign, the one from Selby Street, and the two stolen before July 14th were five different signs.

8. One of the missing signs stood at the corner of Selby Street and Barnacle Road. Selby Street doesn't have any "No Parking" signs.

9. Peabody Lane, which has no "Dead End" signs anywhere near it, intersects with either Dwight Street or Everett Avenue (but not both).

10. The stop sign went missing sometime before the sign at Peabody Lane (but not on July 18th).

	Dead End	No Parking	One Way	Speed Limit	Stop	Yield	Amble Ln.	Barnacle Rd.	Casper Blvd.	Dwight St.	Everett Ave.	Falstaff St.	Oracle Rd.	Peabody Ln.	Quinella St.	Ralston Ave.	Selby St.	Tarragon Ln.
July 4th																		
July 11th																		
July 18th																		
July 25th																		
August 1st																		
August 8th																		
Oracle Rd.																		
Peabody Ln.																		
Quinella St.																		
Ralston Ave.																		
Selby St.																		
Tarragon Ln.																		
Amble Ln.																		
Barnacle Rd.																		
Casper Blvd.																		
Dwight St.																		
Everett Ave.																		
Falstaff St.																		

Dates	Signs	Streets	Streets
July 4th			
July 11th			
July 18th			
July 25th			
August 1st			
August 8th			

Answers on page 254.

COLUMBO

Every word listed is contained within the group of letters. Words can be found in a straight line horizontally, vertically, or diagonally. They may read either forward or backward.

ARREST

BUMBLE

CATCH

CIGAR

COLUMBO

CONFESS

CRIMES

CRIMINAL

CRUMPLED

DETECTIVE

DISHEVELED

FUMBLING

GUILT

HOMICIDE

INCRIMINATE

LAPD

LIEUTENANT

PETER FALK

RAINCOAT

SHABBY

SUSPECT

THE MRS.

```
D R A I N C O A T A R R E S T
P Q W W H L I E U T E N A N T
A W I N C R I M I N A T E K O
L C A C T H E M R S I V C X T
T D C W A E K K J U Z Y D Z L
I P A I C W E V I T C E T E D
V C O K G V T C E P S U S P I
D O L K L A F R E T E P B R W
E N A K M Q R G E K U U U Q V
L F N I T S U J W O J L M S M
P E I T E I T C O L U M B O G
M S M M L D I S H E V E L E D
U S I T S H A B B Y Q I E V O
R R R H S F U E D I C I M O H
C E C B G N I L B M U F U W L
```

Answers on page 254.

POLICE ANAGRAMS

Unscramble each word or phrase below to reveal a word or phrase related to the ranks of police officers.

UNRIPENED TENTS

ESTRANGE

NICE SPORT

AUNTIE LENT

CHOICE FIFE LOP

SOONER MIMICS

I CATNAP

PUT DYE

Answers on page 254.

OVERHEARD INFORMATION PART I

Read the story below, then turn the page and answer the questions.

While on a train, a bystander overheard one man tell another about how best to rob an office. The man said, "Okay, this is the keycard. It's deactivated so it'll show as a temp employee as logging in. Petty cash is in the cube of the CFO's assistant, across from his office, Billy Thompson. She's Renee Thompson, no relation. I think she keeps the cash in the second cabinet drawer. Most of the art is just prints, but there are some good pieces in the CEO's conference room. The extra company laptops that they give out for travel are in the office of the head of IT. She's got a separate code to her office, and I think it's 21-45-93. But if it doesn't work, you can only try again once, because a third wrong try will set off an alarm. And I don't care how much you manage to get or don't get, I get my payment regardless."

OVERHEARD INFORMATION PART II

(Do not read this until you have read the previous page!)
The bystander overheard the information about the crimes that were planned, but didn't have anywhere to write it down! Answer the questions below to help the bystander remember what to tell the police.

1. The keycard will show this employee logging in.
   A. Billy Thompson
   B. Renee Thompson
   C. The head of IT
   D. None of the above

2. Which two employees have the same name but no relation?
   A. The CEO and his assistant
   B. The CFO and his assistant
   C. The CFO and the head of IT
   D. The CEO and the head of IT

Answers on page 255.

3. The code to access the room where spare laptops are kept is:
   A. 45-21-93
   B. 93-21-45
   C. 21-45-93
   D. 22-45-93

4. The man is giving information to the thief because he expects to receive this.
   A. An unspecified payment
   B. A percentage of the haul
   C. A particular piece of art from the CEO's office
   D. He doesn't want a monetary reward, just revenge

SEEN AT THE SCENE
PART I

Study this picture of the crime scene for 1 minute, then turn the page.

SEEN AT THE SCENE PART II

(Do not read this until you have read the previous page!)
Which image exactly matches the picture
from the previous page?

1.

2.

3.

4.

Answer on page 255.

MOTEL HIDEOUT

A thief hides out in one of the 45 motel rooms listed in the chart below. The motel's in-house detective received a sheet of four clues, signed "The Logical Thief." Using these clues, the detective found the room number within 15 minutes—but by that time, the thief had fled. Can you find the thief's motel room more quickly?

1. The number is odd.

2. The number is not a multiple of 3, nor does it have 3 as one of the digits.

3. The number is prime.

4. The sum of the digits is less than 5.

51	52	53	54	55	56	57	58	59
41	42	43	44	45	46	47	48	49
31	32	33	34	35	36	37	38	39
21	22	23	24	25	26	27	28	29
11	12	13	14	15	16	17	18	19

Answer on page 255.

THE MASTER FORGER

A highly-skilled forger appears to be selling "signed" first edition books all over Escambia County. So far five fakes have been discovered, each sold in a different town for a different price, and each by a different author. Help the authorities track down this miscreant by determining the title and author of each book, the town in which it was sold and its final sales price.

1. The five forged items were the two that sold for $325 and $505, the one sold in Palatka, *By the By*, and *Ends & Means*.

2. Of the two books sold in Ocala and Palatka, one went for $370 and the other was Caught Inside.

3. *Ends & Means*, the book sold in Derry, and the book that sold for $325 were by three different authors.

4. The Pam Powell forgery sold for $45 less than the Nick Nells book.

5. Gil Grayson didn't write *Ends & Means*.

6. The Jen Jonson book sold for less money than the forgery that was unloaded at a book shop in West Hills (which wasn't by Pam Powell).

7. The forgery sold in Palatka went for $45 more than the one sold in Micanopy.

8. *At One Time* (which isn't by Jen Jonson) sold for $370.

9. The book by Pam Powell sold for $460.

	At One Time	By the Bay	Caught Inside	Dear Deborah	Ends & Means	Gil Grayson	Harry Haupt	Jen Jonson	Nick Nells	Pam Powell	Derry	Micanopy	Ocala	Palatka	West Hills
Prices															
$325															
$370															
$415															
$460															
$505															
Towns															
Derry															
Micanopy															
Ocala															
Palatka															
West Hills															
Authors															
Gil Grayson															
Harry Haupt															
Jen Jonson															
Nick Nells															
Pam Powell															

Prices	Titles	Authors	Towns
$325			
$370			
$415			
$460			
$505			

Answers on page 255.

TRACK THE FUGITIVE

The investigator is tracking the fugitive's past trips in order to find and recover information that was left behind in five cities. Each city was visited only once. Can you put together the travel timeline, using the information below?

1. Rio de Janeiro was one of the final two cities visited.

2. The trip to Lima happened before the trip to Quito, but at least two other cities separated the visits.

3. From Santiago the fugitive went directly to either Quito or Rio.

4. The fugitive did not begin her travels in Buenos Aires.

5. The fugitive did not travel directly from Chile to Brazil.

Answers on page 255.

THE GEM THIEF

A company that sold gems found that 6 types of gems had been stolen from their warehouse. There was 1 gem of the first type, 2 of the second type, 3 of the third type, 4 of the fourth type, 5 of the fifth type, and 6 of the sixth type. From the information given below, can you tell how many gemstones of each kind were taken?

1. There are four more pearls than diamonds.

2. There are not as many rubies as opals, but rubies are not the least plentiful gem.

3. There are at least 4 amethysts, but they are not the most plentiful gem.

4. There are fewer than 4 sapphires, but they are not the least plentiful gem.

5. There are more rubies than sapphires.

Answers on page 255.

ENTREPRENEURS OF DEATH
PART I

Read this true crime account, then turn to the next page to test your knowledge.

Following the rise of the National Crime Syndicate, or what people now call the Mafia, a group of enterprising killers formed an enforcement arm that a member of the press dubbed "Murder, Incorporated." They were also known as "The Combination" or "The Brownsville Boys," since many of them came from Brooklyn's Brownsville area.

The Combination began their mayhem-for-money operation around 1930 following the formation of the National Crime Syndicate. Until their demise in the mid-1940s, they enforced the rules of organized crime through fear, intimidation, and murder. Most of the group's members were Jewish and Italian gangsters from Brooklyn. The number of murders committed during their bloody reign is unknown even today, but estimates put the total at more than a thousand from coast to coast.

The formation of the group was the brainchild of mob overlords Johnny Torrio and "Lucky" Luciano. The most high-profile assassination credited to the enterprise was the murder of gang lord Dutch Schultz, who defied the syndicate's orders to abandon a plan to assassinate

New York crime-buster Thomas Dewey. The job went to Charles "Charlie the Bug" Workman, whose bloody prowess ranked alongside such Murder, Inc., elite as Louis "Lepke" Buchalter, the man who issued the orders; Albert Anastasia, the lord high executioner; Abe "Kid Twist" Reles, whose eventual capitulation led to the group's downfall; Louis Capone (no relation to Al); Frank Abbandando; Harry "Pittsburg Phil" Strauss, an expert with an ice pick; Martin "Buggsy" Goldstein; Harry "Happy" Maione, leader of the Italian faction; Irving "Knadles" Nitzberg, who twice beat a death sentence when his convictions were overturned; Vito "Socko" Gurino; Jacob Drucker; Philip "Little Farvel" Cohen; and Sholom Bernstein, who like many of his cohorts turned against his mentors to save his own life. It was an era of infamy unequaled in mob lore.

Known as "Kid Twist," Abe Reles may not have been as bloodthirsty as some of his contemporaries, but he was cursed with a huge ego and a big mouth, and he wasn't shy about doing his bragging in front of cops, judges, the press, or the public at large. When an informant fingered Reles and "Buggsy" Goldstein for the murder of a small-time hood, both men turned themselves in, believing they could beat the rap just as they had a dozen times before, but this one was ironclad. Reles sang loud and clear, implicating his peers and bosses in more than 80 murders and sending several of them to the electric chair, including the untouchable Buchalter.

ENTREPRENEURS OF DEATH
PART II

(Do not read this until you have read the previous page!)

1. The name "Murder, Incorporated" came from this source.

    A. The police

    B. The Brownsville Boys themselves

    C. A member of the press

    D. Al Capone

2. The Combination are believed to be responsible for about this many deaths.

    A. 120

    B. 500

    C. 1,000

    D. 3,400

3. This member was an "expert with an ice pick."

    A. Louis Capone

    B. Harry Strauss

    C. Abe Reles

    D. Albert Anastasia

4. Reles was arrested along with this other man.

    A. "Buggsy" Goldstein

    B. Louis "Lepke" Buchalter

    C. "Lucky" Luciano

    D. Sholom Bernstein

Answers on page 255.

DNA SEQUENCE

Examine the two images below carefully. Are these sequences a match or not?

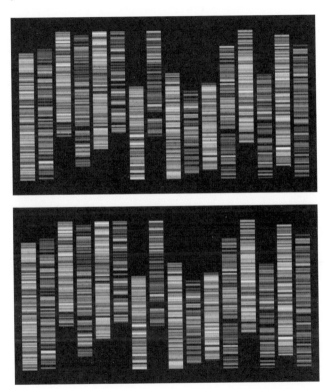

Answer on page 256.

INTERCEPTION

You've intercepted a message between a criminal who fled and his accomplice. But the message doesn't seem to make sense! Can you discover the criminal's current location hidden in the message?

TART HUH REAR ERE PEER

PEP BUMMER

THREAT PURR AREA SKIING NOUN

BITTER ROOT

BUSSING ARIA ANNO BADDER DICING REED GORGE SOON

Answer on page 256.

A LONG PATH FROM CRIME TO TRIAL

Change just one letter on each line to go from the top word to the bottom word. Do not change the order of the letters. You must have an English word at each step.

CRIME

_____

_____

_____

_____

_____

_____ sets of two

_____

_____

_____

_____

_____

_____

_____

TRIAL

Answers on page 256.

ROBERT B. PARKER BOOKS

ACROSS

1. Apt anagram of "notes"

6. Be a braggart

11. Folded Mexican snacks

12. Award named for Poe

13. Spenser and Hawk battle a street gang in the 19th Spenser novel

15. Balcony section

16. Barely squeeze by (with "out")

17. Suffer from overexercise, maybe

20. In literature, Pussycat's friend

22. Life force, in Taoism

23. Like the Cheshire Cat

27. Eighth novel about Parker's Massachusetts cop Jesse Stone

29. Bouncing off the walls

30. Back talk

31. "The Whiffenpoof Song" singer

32. Hair styling substances

33. Charged particle

36. Narrow wood strip

38. Parker's sixth book about his lady private eye Sunny Randall

43. Gold fabrics

44. Boris, to Bullwinkle

45. Vote in

46. Dull photo finish

DOWN

1. Norm, for short

2. "The Way" of Lao Tzu

3. Bygone French coin

4. Barnes's business partner

5. Home to the Kon-Tiki Museum

6. Moistening

7. Admiring poem

8. Dickensian chill

9. Drop the quarterback

10. Yuletide buy

14. More than a swellhead

17. Adolescent woe

18. Fashionable and stylish

19. Like a soprano's voice

21. Lawyer's deg.

23. Most quiet
24. Like a loafer
25. Get just right
26. Hoodwinks
28. Clod buster
32. Accra's nation
33. It is surrounded by water
34. Gem for a Scorpio, perhaps
35. Rumpelstiltskin's secret
37. Opponent of "us"
39. Red VCR button
40. Fish tank accessory
41. Basic time standard: Abbr.
42. CBS symbol

1	2	3	4	5	■	6	7	8	9	10
11					■	12				
13					14					
■	■	15					■	16		
17	18	19		■	20		21	■	■	■
22			■	23				24	25	26
27			28							
29							■	30		
■	■	31			■	32				
33	34	35	■	36		37			■	■
38			39					40	41	42
43				■	44					
45				■	46					

Answers on page 256.

BLUE BLOODS

Every word listed is contained within the group of letters. Words can be found in a straight line horizontally, vertically, or diagonally. They may read either forward or backward.

ARREST

ATTORNEY

BLUE

CHARGE

CITY

COMMISSIONER

COPS

DANNY

DETECTIVE

ERIN

FAMILY

FRANK

HENRY

JAMIE

JUSTICE

LINDA

MOYNAHAN (Bridget)

NYPD

OFFICER

POLICE

REAGAN

SELLECK (Tom)

WAHLBERG (Donnie)

```
A Y R E N O I S S I M M O C G
E R I N H J W A H L B E R G R
K B E E A M J S E L L E C K Z
Y A N M K E J E F A M I L Y D
H R I W E V E C I L O P A T P
Y E S E F I C O P S Y I T I Y
H A O G R T M T K T N R T C N
L G Y R A C O A D X A Z O J N
G A J A N E P T L G H V R U O
W N B H K T S Y N N A D N S F
I J B C A E F Y R O N L E T F
W U X L R D G C D D S V Y I I
Q U Q R U U N B S V Y J H C C
B J A O P E S I Z U Z H K E E
W N S O K M K D L X X Y T Q R
```

Answers on page 256.

ANSWERS

CRIME ABBREVIATIONS AND ACRONYMS
(page 4)

1. A; 2. C; 3. C; 4. A

FIRST STEAL, THEN FLEE
(page 5)

Answers may vary. STEAL, steel, steep, sleep, sleet, fleet, FLEES

FITTING WORDS
(page 6)

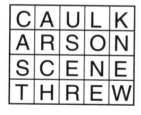

C	A	U	L	K
A	R	S	O	N
S	C	E	N	E
T	H	R	E	W

LAW AND DISORDER
(page 7)

1. Paper clutter on desk replaced with a crossword puzzle; 2. the days have been stolen from the calendar; 3. spittoon is missing; 4. hole in shoe sole has been repaired; 5. sheriff's mustache is missing; 6. sheriff's badge is missing; 7. incandescent bulb in the overhead light has been replaced by a modern eco-friendly fluorescent bulb; 8. "reward" on the poster now reads "drawer"; 9. one chair leg is gone

CRIME SCENE
(page 8)

¹S	²T	³A	⁴I	R		⁶S	⁷P	⁸O	⁹R	¹⁰T
¹¹O	U	I	D	A		¹²A	R	M	O	R
¹³D	N	A	E	V	¹⁴I	D	E	N	C	E
			¹⁵E	A	R	L		¹⁶E	S	E
¹⁷A	¹⁸H	¹⁹A		²⁰G	O	Y	²¹A			
²²L	A	W	²³M	E	N		²⁴M	²⁵I	²⁶N	²⁷T
²⁸B	L	O	O	D		²⁹F	I	B	E	R
³⁰S	O	L	D		³¹M	E	D	I	C	O
			³²E	³³G	A	D		³⁴S	K	Y
³⁵I	³⁶T	³⁷S		³⁸O	³⁹R	E	S			
⁴⁰P	H	O	T	O	G	R	A	⁴²P	⁴³H	⁴⁴S
⁴⁵S	E	R	I	F		⁴⁶A	R	E	A	S
⁴⁷E	N	E	M	Y		⁴⁸L	A	R	G	E

ANSWERS

A BLOODY DEATH
(page 10)

VEIN, veil, veal, real, reap, leap, lead, DEAD

ORDER IN THE COURT
(page 11)

1	2	3	4	5	6	7	8	9	10	11	12	13
T	R	I	A	L	S	E	Z	X	J	N	M	Y
14	15	16	17	18	19	20	21	22	23	24	25	26
U	Q	D	B	O	P	C	F	G	H	V	W	K

SPY SCRAMBLE
(page 12)

1.Buenos Aires, last flight; 2.Singapore, sunrise; 3.Sydney, eleven AM; 4. Chicago, midnight; 5. Johannesburg fifteen hundred hours

MOTEL HIDEOUT
(page 13)

The thief is in room 11.

THE SOPRANOS
(page 14)

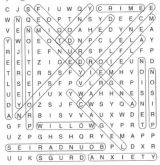

TYPES OF EVIDENCE (PART II)
(page 18)

1. True; 2. False. Palynology is the science that studies plant spores, insects, seeds, and other microorganisms. 3. False. 4. True. 5. True.

FIND THE WITNESS
(page 19)

Jenkins lives in house E.

ANSWERS

WEAPON WORDS
(page 20)

1. bomb; 2. bullet; 3. arrow;
4. rifle; 5. sword

CRYPTOKU
(page 21)

I	B	T	H	E	N	A	K	S
E	K	A	S	B	I	H	T	N
N	H	S	T	K	A	B	E	I
K	E	I	A	T	S	N	B	H
B	A	N	K	H	E	I	S	T
S	T	H	N	I	B	K	A	E
A	N	E	I	S	K	T	H	B
H	I	B	E	A	T	S	N	K
T	S	K	B	N	H	E	I	A

THRILLING READS
(page 24)

¹T	²I	³A	⁴R	⁵A		⁶M	⁷U	⁸K	L	⁹U	¹⁰K
¹²A	T	L	A	S		¹³E	L	A	I	N	E
¹⁴C	R	O	S	S	¹⁵C	O	U	N	T	R	Y
¹⁶T	Y	P	H	O	O	N			¹⁷T	O	N
			¹⁸E	R	S		¹⁹A	²⁰D	E	L	E
²¹K	²²I	²³S	S	T	H	²⁴E	G	I	R	L	S
²⁵E	T	A	T	S		²⁶B	E	N			
²⁷B	A	G			²⁸A	R	I	E	²⁹T	³⁰T	³¹A
³²A	L	E	³³X	³⁴C	R	O	S	S	R	U	N
³⁵B	I	L	L	E	T		³⁶T	E	E	N	A
³⁷S	A	Y	S	O	S		³⁸S	N	E	E	S

WHAT'S THE CRIME?
(page 26)

insider trading

PARKING TICKETS
(page 22)

Times	Models	Colors	Locations
10:00am	Nissan	black	Sandy St.
11:00am	Chevrolet	silver	Apple Ave.
12:00pm	Mazda	brown	Tawny Terr.
1:00pm	Honda	green	Raffle Rd.
2:00pm	Toyota	blue	Lantern Ln.

WHAT'S THE CRIME?
(page 26)

Credit card fraud

ANSWERS

THE GEM THIEF
(page 27)

The count is: 1 piece of topaz, 2 pearls, 3 rubies, 4 sapphires, and 5 diamonds.

TRACK THE FUGITIVE
(page 28)

The order is: Las Vegas, Portland, Montpelier, Pensacola, and Indianapolis

A FAMOUS ATTEMPT
(page 29)

Frank Morris and brothers Clarence and John Anglin escaped Alcatraz prison in 1962, when they were all in their 30s. While they are believed to have drowned, the case has never been officially closed.

WHODUNIT?
(page 30)

MUG – (G) + BIRD – (BI) + BEER – (BE) + ARMY – (AR) + LIST – (LI) + E + FRY – C = MURDER MYSTERY

OVERHEARD INFORMATION (PART II)
(page 32)

1. A; 2. B; 3. C; 4. D

SEEN AT THE SCENE (PART II)
(page 34)

Picture 1 is a match.

ANSWERS

PICK YOUR POISON
(page 35)

From left to right, the bottles are purple, brown, white, yellow, and blue. The poison is found in the brown bottle.

DNA SEQUENCE
(page 36)

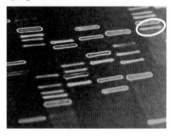

THE SUSPECT FLED TO...
(page 37)

1	2	3	4	5	6	7	8	9	10	11	12	13
G	S	W	I	T	Z	E	R	L	A	N	D	H
14	15	16	17	18	19	20	21	22	23	24	25	26
P	Y	Q	K	U	J	X	C	V	B	M	O	F

SPY SCRAMBLE
(page 38)

forest preserve mile marker ten

MOTEL HIDEOUT
(page 39)

The thief is in room 22.

STOLEN ART
(page 40)

ANSWERS

INTERCEPTION
(page 42)

Take the first letter of each word to reveal: Charlotte, NC (North Carolina)

WHAT DO YOU SEE? (PART II)
(page 44)

Picture 3 is a match.

NO BONES ABOUT IT
(page 45)

1. d) rhomboid

2. c) pointal

3. b) paella

4. c) perpendicular

5. d) porkal

6. a) vertical

7. d) pimpal

8. b) capital

KEEPING THE PEACE
(page 46)

CLAW - (C) + HAND - (H) + SWORD - (SW) + ARCHER - (ARCH) = LAW AND ORDER

FIND THE WITNESS
(page 47)

The Banks live in house A.

POLICE DISPATCHER
(page 48)

Times	Officers	Calls	Locations
8:45am	Neville	bank robbery	Midtown
9:30am	Harry	alarm	Downtown
10:15am	Linda	stolen car	Bus. District
11:00am	Jeffrey	trespassing	South End
11:45am	Dale	cat in tree	Uptown
12:30pm	Brenda	accident	North End

ANSWERS

CRIME ON TV
(page 50)

B	O	N	E	S		P	A	I	L	S
O	D	I	S	T		A	S	N	I	T
M	E	C	C	A		T	I	A	R	A
B	R	E	A	K	I	N	G	B	A	D
		P	I	S	A	N	O			.
S	I	R	E	N	S			O	L	E
Q	U	E	E	G		S	S	T	A	R
S	M	L			U	T	A	H	A	N
	E	M	I	N	E	M				
S	E	A	R	C	H	P	A	R	T	Y
I	T	S	M	E		O	R	U	R	O
G	R	E	E	R		F	R	E	A	K
N	E	S	T	S		F	A	R	G	O

THE GEM THIEF
(page 52)

The count is: 1 peridot, 2 emeralds, 3 pieces of jade, 4 aquamarines, and 5 pearls.

PICK YOUR POISON
(page 53)

From left to right, the bottles are red (1), orange, red (2), pink. The poison is found in the orange bottle.

A SUCCESSFUL DISAPPEARANCE
(page 54)

Eleanor Jarman, born in Iowa, disappeared at the age of 39. In 1933, Jarman, her boyfriend, and another man tried to rob a clothing store. Jarman's accomplice shot the store owner. Jarman served seven years in prison before she escaped to see her family. From there she disappeared, communicating with her family via newspaper ads.

ANSWERS

DNA SEQUENCE
(page 55)

They are a match.

TO THE LETTER
(page 56)

pursue, purse

CROSSED WORDS
(page 56)

protect/serve

MOTEL HIDEOUT
(page 57)

The thief is in room 56.

POISON!
(PART II)
(page 60)

1. False. 2. False. 3. False.
4. True. 5. True

SEEN AT THE SCENE
(PART II)
(page 62)

Picture 3 is a match.

CRIME ANAGRAMS
(page 63)

distribution; solicitation; tax evasion; vandalism; shop-lifting; harassment; stalking; wire fraud

TRACK THE FUGITIVE
(page 64)

The order is: Tokyo, Santiago, Algiers, Berlin, Lisbon

FINGERPRINT MATCH
(page 65)

E is the matching fingerprint.

ANSWERS

IN SEARCH OF EVIDENCE
(page 66)

E	R	S	E		C	A	R		I	T	I	S
	O	U	T	S	I	D	E		R	A	G	E
	D	N	A	P	R	O	F	I	L	I	N	G
P	E	R		E	C	R	U			G	I	O
A	N	O		C	E	N	T		E	A	T	S
S	T	O	A	T			E	M	T		E	
A		F	O	R	E	N	S	I	C	S		T
	S		N	A	S			T	H	E	S	E
D	A	M	E		C	L	E	O		A	E	R
E	M	I		O	A	R	S		S	L	R	
F	I	N	G	E	R	P	R	I	N	T	S	
A	T	T	A		T	U	E	S	D	A	Y	
T	E	S	T		S	P	D		A	R	N	E

CRYPTO-LOGIC
(page 68)

TRICKERY

OVERHEARD INFORMATION (PART II)
(page 70)

1. B; 2. A; 3. B; 4. C

WILL THE PERP GO TO JAIL?
(page 71)

Answers may vary. PERP, perk, park, pack, tack, talk, tall, tail, JAIL

THE GEM THIEF
(page 72)

The count is: 1 diamond, 2 emeralds, 3 rubies, 4 opals, and 5 garnets.

INTERCEPTION
(page 73)

Take the last letter of each word to reveal: Meet Monday Rogers Park

ANSWERS

CRYPTO-LOGIC
(page 74)

DECEPTIVE

FOND OF ROBBING BANKS
(page 75)

A bank robber of the 1940s and 1950s, Frederick Grant Dunn was called "the Modern John Dillinger." After an escape from custody in 1958, he was added to the Most Wanted List. He was found dead from causes unknown in 1959.

THE JUDGE
(page 76)

Sentences	Defendants	Crimes	Lawyers
1 month	Rachel	grand theft	McFerry
2 months	Frederick	ID theft	Barrett
4 months	Annabelle	perjury	Oswald
8 months	Nelson	shoplifting	Zimmerman
16 months	Jasmine	assault	Colson

THE "MOST HATED MAN IN THE WORLD"
(page 78)

THE BODY FARM (PART II)
(page 82)

1. False. 2. True. 3. True. 4. True. 5. False

SEEN AT THE SCENE (PART II)
(page 84)

Picture 3 is a match.

ANSWERS

MOTEL HIDEOUT
(page 85)

The thief is in room 53.

FBI QUIZ
(page 86)

1. C; 2. C; 3. D; 4. C

TRACK THE FUGITIVE
(page 87)

The order is: Riga, Oslo, Zagreb, Madrid, Warsaw

THE SHOPLIFTER
(page 88)

Days	Items	Stores	Locations
Sunday	drill	Nell HQ	First St.
Monday	jacket	City Shop	Underhill Rd.
Tuesday	cologne	Greentail	D St.
Wednesday	sunglasses	Totopia	Little Ln.
Thursday	bracelet	Dellmans	Prince Ave.

EITHER/OR
(page 90)

decent con / connected

EITHER/OR
(page 90)

least / steal

DNA SEQUENCE
(page 91)

They are a match.

THE CASE OF THE DISAPPEARING GEMS
(page 92)

1	2	3	4	5	6	7	8	9	10	11	12	13
J	A	D	E		C	N	Q	K	V		R	U	B	Y

14	15	16	17	18	19	20	21	22	23	24	25	26
M	Z	T	L	G	X	F	S	O	P	H	I	W

WHAT CHANGED? (PART II)
(page 94)

The frying pan flipped.

ANSWERS

MURDER IN NEW ORLEANS
(page 95)

In 1918 and 1919, a man with an axe terrorized New Orleans with his murders in the Italian-American community. His murder spree stopped abruptly, leaving the case unsolved forever.

MASTER OF MYSTERY
(page 96)

PICK YOUR POISON
(page 98)

From left to right, the bottles are purple, green, orange, red, and teal. The poison is found in the green bottle.

FIND THE WITNESS
(page 99)

Brown lives in house E.

REMEMBERING THE SCENE (PART II)
(page 102)

1. C; 2. False; 3. False; 4. False; 5. B; 6. C

SEEN AT THE SCENE (PART II)
(page 104)

Picture 4 is a match.

THE GEM THIEF
(page 105)

The count is: 1 turquoise, 2 pieces of jade, 3 amethysts, 4 sapphires, and 5 pearls.

ANSWERS

TRACK THE FUGITIVE
(page 106)

The order is: La Paz, Panama City, Caracas, Quito, Montevideo

INTERCEPTION
(page 107)

Take the first and last letter of each word and you will reveal: Inside orange vase

JUST ONE MORE HEIST
(page 108)

DANNY, dandy, handy, hands, bands, bends, beads, brads, grads, goads, goats, coats, chats, chaws, chews, chess, chest, cheat, cleat, clean, olean, OCEAN

OVERHEARD INFORMATION (PART II)
(page 110)

1. A; 2. B; 3. B; 4. A

CRIME QUIZ
(page 111)

1. Dead body; 2. Last name unknown; 3. Gunshot wound; 4. Department of Corrections; 5. Attempt to locate

THE CAR THIEF
(page 112)

Years	Models	Owners	Towns
1966	Continental	Thomas	Ridgewood
1969	Thunderbird	Irving	Deerfield
1972	Mustang	Dennis	Taunton
1975	Camaro	Jennifer	Montclair
1978	Corvette	Beatrice	Kearney

ANSWERS

WOMEN IN BLUE
(page 114)

HISTORICAL MURDERERS
(page 116)

MOTEL HIDEOUT
(page 118)

The thief is in room 41.

SEEN AT THE SCENE
(PART II)
(page 120)

Picture 2 is a match.

CRIME ANAGRAMS
(page 121)

burglary; grand theft auto; accessory; bribery; manslaughter; conspiracy; racketeering; possession

TRACK THE FUGITIVE
(page 122)

The order is: Butte, Cleveland, Des Moines, San Diego, Sacramento

ANSWERS

IT'S IN THE BLOOD (PART II)
(page 124)

1. A+; 2. O-; 3. AB+; 4. AB-;
5. True

MURDER IN COLORADO
(page 125)

The Denver Strangler killed up to five women between 1894 and 1903. The killer may have murdered a clairvoyant who had supposedly given information to the authorities; she was found dead, strangled. Although several men were suspects, the Denver Strangler was never identified.

DNA SEQUENCE
(page 126)

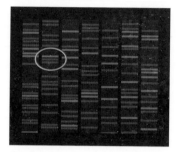

THE SUSPECT FLED TO...
(page 127)

1	2	3	4	5	6	7	8	9	10	11	12	13
H	J	O	C	P	A	R	I	S	D	V	F	K

14	15	16	17	18	19	20	21	22	23	24	25	26
Q	Y	N	Z	E	U	T	B	X	M	G	W	L

INTERCEPTION
(page 128)

Take the center letter of each place name and you will reveal that the criminal is hidden in Iowa.

ANSWERS

WHAT CHANGED? (PART II)
(page 130)

Evidence markers 8, 9, and 10 have disappeared from the scene.

DETECTIVE WORK!
(page 131)

The stolen items are the hook, the fish bone, and the bear head. These items are circled on the easel.

A CRIMINALLY GOOD QUOTE
(page 132)

Missing letters spell: "I rob banks because that's where the money is."

TRACK THE FUGITIVE
(page 134)

The order is: Seoul, Dodoma, Skopje, Riyadh, Stockholm

MOTEL HIDEOUT
(page 135)

The thief is in room 17.

ANSWERS

EITHER/OR
(page 136)

wanders / wardens

SHOPLIFTING
(page 136)

Answers may vary. SHOP, shot, soot, soft, sift, LIFT

SEEN AT THE SCENE (PART II)
(page 138)

Picture 1 is a match.

CRIME QUIZ
(page 139)

1. Breaking and entering;
2. Assault with a deadly weapon; 3. Driving while intoxicated; 4. Failure to appear; 5. Grand theft auto

THE EMBEZZLER
(page 140)

Amounts	Companies	Locations	Industries
$500,000	Melcisco	Atlanta	web hosting
$1,000,000	Wexica Inc.	Chicago	telephony
$2,000,000	Truetel	New York	mobile apps
$4,000,000	Dynacorp	Portland	logistics
$8,000,000	Centrafour	Boston	microchips

THE BURKE AND HARE MURDERS
(page 142)

ANSWERS

MURDER IN UTAH
(page 144)

Francis Hermann was a pastor—and a murderer. Born circa 1850, he moved to the United States from England. His first two wives died under suspicious circumstances. Hermann later murdered two women in Salt Lake City. Not long after their deaths, he fled Salt Lake City and escaped justice, evading capture.

DNA SEQUENCE
(page 145)

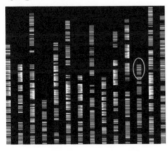

FINGERPRINT MATCH
(page 146)

E, L, and N are the matching fingerprints.

PICK YOUR POISON
(page 147)

From left to right, the bottles are red, blue, orange, green, and yellow. The poison is found in the yellow bottle.

INTERCEPTION
(page 148)

Take the first letter of each word to reveal: Train Depot, Five AM

FIND THE WITNESS (PART II)
(page 149)

Shah lives in house A.

ANSWERS

A CASE OF ARSON
(page 152)

1. Unlikely. Turpentine was used as an accelerant, and it was not stored in the office. 2. False. 3. Unconfirmed. Greene had returned the keycard issued by the company, but he could have duplicated it prior to leaving. 4. True, his girlfriend. 5. Unconfirmed, as the only word for this was his own.

MOTEL HIDEOUT
(page 153)

The thief is in room 49.

FORGING MONEY
(page 154)

Answers may vary. FORGE, forte, forts, fores, bores, bones, hones, honey, MONEY

SEEN AT THE SCENE (PART II)
(page 156)

Picture 1 is a match.

CRIME ANAGRAMS
(page 157)

prosecutor; attorney; defendant; jury trial; witness; bailiffs; plaintiff; grand jury

THE GEM THIEF
(page 158)

The count is: 1 piece of topaz, 2 amethysts, 3 pieces of jade, 4 peridots, 5 emeralds, and 6 opals.

TRACK THE FUGITIVE
(page 159)

The order is: Moscow, Tunis, Athens, Brussels, Ankara

ANSWERS

MURDER METHODS
(page 160)

```
K  A  M  O  E  T  I  H  A  X  A  N  D  E
C  R  I  C  T  I  M  P  A  L  E  J  R  X
N  S  Q  O  O  E  D  M  H  P  A  O  F  P
O  O  T  Z  R  Z  E  L  H  A  G  R  O  E
O  N  A  B  R  K  N  G  S  T  W  I  D  S
R  M  E  H  A  J  P  P  P  M  S  O  S  N
F  E  B  S  G  T  H  A  P  O  L  U  S  R
O  X  H  I  H  Y  S  E  N  P  V  L  T  J
M  E  Y  T  X  O  J  H  X  M  Y  Z  R  A
Y  X  J  X  O  X  O  E  T  O  P  G  A  P
N  P  A  Z  L  M  J  T  U  J  Y  A  N  M
W  T  V  O  B  P  S  B  Q  J  R  Q  G  Z
E  G  G  U  I  L  L  O  T  I  N  E  L  O
M  Y  G  T  Q  P  R  E  W  E  K  S  E  W
```

DNA SEQUENCE
(page 162)

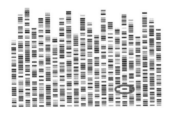

WHAT DO YOU SEE? (PART II)
(page 164)

Picture 3 is a match.

INTERVIEWING WITNESSES
(page 165)

Since A is telling the truth, we know C is lying when saying that B is a truth teller. Therefore D must be the second truth teller.

THE DOGNAPPER
(page 166)

Days	Breeds	Dogs	Families
Monday	Pomeranian	Terry	McHale
Tuesday	Rottweiler	Kenzie	Albertson
Wednesday	Great Dane	Lucille	Voigt
Thursday	Chihuahua	Benji	Singh
Friday	Bulldog	Fido	Jenkins

ANSWERS

NOT QUITE A WANTED POSTER

Famous for the corruption in his political machine, William "Boss" Tweed fled to Spain while on house arrest. He was caught because someone there recognized him due to political cartoons that skewered his corrupt "Tammany Hall" machine.

WHAT CHANGED? (PART II)
(page 170)

A binder disappeared.

INTERCEPTION
(page 171)

Take the last letter of each word to reveal: Bus station, Six PM

TRIAL OF THE CENTURY (1927 EDITION) (PART II)
(page 174)

1. A. Albert; 2. B. A tie clip with his initials; 3. C. The Blonde Butcher; 4. A. Lorraine

SEEN AT THE SCENE (PART II)
(page 176)

1. C. 1, 2, 3, 5; 2. A. On; 3. Off; 4. B. No

MOTEL HIDEOUT
(page 177)

The thief is in room 14.

ANSWERS

THE GEM THIEF
(page 178)

The count is: 1 sapphire, 2 agates, 3 pearls, 4 turquoises, 5 rubies, and 6 diamonds.

TRACK THE FUGITIVE
(page 179)

The order is: Paris, Vienna, Stockholm, Vaduz, Berlin

POLICE LINEUPS
(page 180)

WHEN YOU DON'T WANT YOUR 15 MINUTES OF FAME
(page 182)

The subject of the very first episode of the television show "America's Most Wanted" in 1988, David James Roberts hid in his apartment for four days after seeing his case profiled on television. Among other crimes, Roberts was convicted of armed robbery and murder.

OVERHEARD INFORMATION (PART II)
(page 184)

1. A. A bakery; 2. A. February 8; 3. A. February 8. The theft will only be delayed if it snows; 4. D. Fourth

CRIME ANAGRAMS
(page 185)

assault; perpetrator; misdemeanor; probable cause; infraction; narcotics; inmate; probation

CRIME QUIZ
(page 186)

1. Be on the lookout; 2. All points bulletin; 3. Known associate; 4. District Attorney; 5. Unknown subject

WHAT CHANGED? (PART II)
(page 188)

A pair of tweezers disappeared. Look to the right of the scissors in the bottom half of the suitcase.

LOOPY LAWS
(page 189)

According to Rich Smith in "You Can Get Arrested for That," it's illegal to fall asleep in a cheese factory in South Dakota.

ISABELLA'S MISSING COLLECTION
(page 190)

THE PONZI SCHEMERS
(page 192)

Years	Assets	Headquarters	Hedge Funds
2007	$50 million	Chicago	Alpha Sky
2010	$32 million	Los Angeles	Wellspring
2013	$225 million	Seattle	Gemstone
2016	$79 million	Miami	Concorde
2019	$105 million	Dallas	Goldleaf

ANSWERS

DNA SEQUENCE
(page 194)

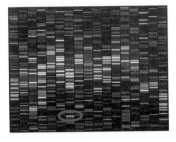

PICK YOUR POISON
(page 195)

From left to right, the bottles are blue (1), yellow, blue (2), orange, purple, and red. The poison is found in the yellow bottle.

INTERCEPTION
(page 196)

Take the second letter of each word to reveal: Redeye flight to LA

FIND THE WITNESS
(page 197)

Ken Rawlins and his wife are found in house E.

MAKING A LIST, CHECKING IT TWICE
(page 198)

William Kinsey Hutchinson was the editor-in-chief for the International News Service when he had a conversation with J. Edgar Hoover. The FBI Ten Most Wanted Fugitive List was born from that discussion. Years earlier, Hutchinson had also been a reporter at the famous Scopes trial.

FEMALE BANK ROBBERS (PART II)
(page 200)

1. B. 5%; 2. A. Parker; 3. D. Machine Gun Molly; 4. C. 1960s

ANSWERS

MOTEL HIDEOUT
(page 201)

The thief is in room 57.

THE GEM THIEF
(page 202)

The count is: 1 opal, 2 garnets, 3 aquamarines, 4 emeralds, 5 pieces of topaz, and 6 pieces of jade.

TRACK THE FUGITIVE
(page 203)

The order is: Dallas, Denver, Portland, Austin, Nashville

THE GRAFFITI GANG
(page 204)

Tags	Name	Neighborhood	Colors
15	Lucretia	Uptown	orange & teal
22	Daryl	West Side	gray & purple
29	Patrick	East Side	cyan & silver
36	Clarence	Downtown	green & white
43	Agatha	Midtown	blue & pink

STOLEN STREET SIGNS
(page 206)

Dates	Signs	Streets	Streets
July 4th	One Way	Dwight St.	Ralston Ave.
July 11th	Speed Limit	Casper Blvd.	Tarragon Ln.
July 18th	Dead End	Amble Ln.	Quinella St.
July 25th	Yield	Barnacle Rd.	Selby St.
August 1st	Stop	Falstaff St.	Oracle Rd.
August 8th	No Parking	Everett Ave.	Peabody Ln.

COLUMBO
(page 208)

```
D R A I N C O A T A R R E S T
P Q W W H L I E U T E N A N T
A W I N C R I M I N A T E K O
L C A C T H E M R S I V C X T
T D C W A E K K J U Z Y D Z L
I P A C W E V I T C E T E D
V C O K G V T C E P S U S P I
D O L K L A F R E T E P B R W
E N A K M Q R G E K U U U Q V
L F N I T S U J W O J L M S M
P E I T E I T C O L U M B O G
M S M M L D I S H E V E L E D
U S I T S H A B B Y Q I E V O
R R R H S F U E D I C I M O H
C E C B G N I L B M U F U W L
```

POLICE ANAGRAMS
(page 210)

superintendent; sergeant; inspector; lieutenant; chief of police; commissioner; captain; deputy

ANSWERS

OVERHEARD INFORMATION (PART II)
(page 212)

1. D. None of the above; 2. B. The CFO and his assistant; 3. C. 21-45-93; 4. A. An unspecified payment

SEEN AT THE SCENE (PART II)
(page 214)

Picture 4 is a match.

MOTEL HIDEOUT
(page 215)

The answer is 11.

THE MASTER FORGER
(page 216)

Prices	Titles	Authors	Towns
$325	Dear Deborah	Jen Jonson	Micanopy
$370	At One Time	Gil Grayson	Palatka
$415	Ends & Means	Harry Haupt	West Hills
$460	By the Bay	Pam Powell	Derry
$505	Caught Inside	Nick Nells	Ocala

TRACK THE FUGITIVE
(page 218)

The order is: Lima, Buenos Aires, Santiago, Quito, Rio de Janeiro

THE GEM THIEF
(page 219)

The count is: 1 diamond, 2 sapphires, 3 rubies, 4 amethysts, 5 pearls, and 6 opals.

ENTREPRENEURS OF DEATH (PART II)
(page 222)

1. C. A member of the press; 2. C. 1,000; 3. B. Harry Strauss; 4. A. "Buggsy" Goldstein

ANSWERS

DNA SEQUENCE
(page 223)

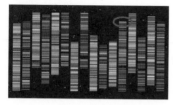

INTERCEPTION
(page 224)

In each word, find the letter that occurs twice, and you end up with: Three PM train to San Diego

A LONG PATH FROM CRIME TO TRIAL
(page 225)

Answers may vary. CRIME, grime, gripe, grips, grins, gains, pains, pairs, hairs, hairy, dairy, daily, drily, drill, trill, TRIAL

ROBERT B. PARKER BOOKS
(page 226)

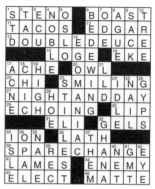

BLUE BLOODS
(page 228)